CW00925442

Along the
Fife Coastal Path

THE FIFE COASTAL PATH

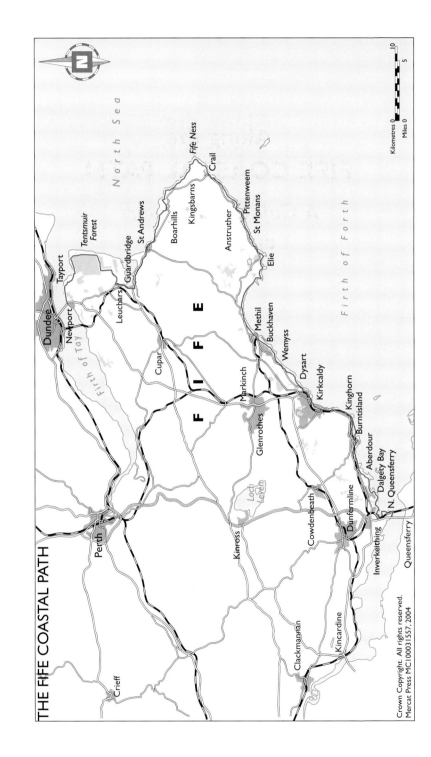

N

North Sea

Dundee
Tayport
Newport
Tentsmuir Forest
Guardbridge
St Andrews
Leuchars
Boarhills
Kingsbarns
Fife Ness
Crail
Cupar
Anstruther
Pittenweem
St Monans
Elie
Markinch
Methil
Buckhaven
Wemyss
Dysart
Kirkcaldy
Glenrothes
Kinghorn
Burntisland
Aberdour
Dalgety Bay
N. Queensferry
Loch Leven
Cowdenbeath
Kinross
Dunfermline
Inverkeithing
Queensferry
Perth
Crieff
Clackmannan
Kincardine

Firth of Tay

Firth of Forth

F I F E

Kilometres 0   10
Miles 0   5

Along the
FIFE COASTAL PATH

A Guide for Walkers
and Visitors

Hamish Brown

mercatpress
www.mercatpress.com

First published in 2004 by Mercat Press Ltd.
10 Coates Crescent, Edinburgh EH3 7AL
www.mercatpress.com

Cartography by MapSet Ltd, Newcastle upon Tyne
Reproduced by permission of Ordnance Survey on behalf of
The Controller of Her Majesty's Stationery Office
© Crown copyright 100031557

ISBN: 184183 0577

Set in Gill Sans and Palatino at Mercat Press

Printed in Spain by Graficas Santamaria

CONTENTS

Maps

INTRODUCTION

People have *walked* on the Fife coast for millennia, whether on business, travel, pilgrimage or pleasure, and if packmen no longer ply their trade and miners no longer tramp to and from their labours, then today we are seeing a growing number of people walking for recreation. Half of Scotland's population lies within an hour's drive of the Fife coast, and good rail and road systems bring it within easy reach of the rest of the world!

It was James VI who described Scotland as 'a beggar's mantle fringed with gold', and you won't be allowed to stay ignorant that the fringe was the Fife coast and the gold the export trade from its ports and later the fishing industry. Not much of this prosperity survives. If the salt panning died two centuries ago and industries like shale oil, linen and coal mining (in my lifetime) have followed, then one gain has been ours, as the squalor of such industries is replaced with rural regeneration and urban renewal. Tourism is big business now, which is one reason the Fife Coastal Path has been developed. Walking a route like this, we actually put our money where our feet are!

The non-walking visitor will find this a useful guide for the towns and sites that dangle like beads on the Fife fringe, but I hope it encourages such to do some walking as well, linking places of interest afoot and so discovering the great benefit to wellbeing that comes from walking. Sir Walter Scott, when work drove him to despair, would go for a good long walk 'to regain his elasticity of mind'.

There is nothing to beat exploring on foot, and the natural linear progression of following a coast also means transport is fairly straightforward, so one can travel to a town, walk, and then, at the day's end, be able to return easily to the start. The whole coast could be explored piecemeal like this but, as advocated before, how much more rewarding to win free of the wheeled monsters and for a week or two go footloose and fancy free along the Castles Coast and East Neuk. If you are a walker this is obvious, if you are a nascent walker there's no place better to give 'real' walking a try.

For most of the time the route is obvious. Navigation is simplified: the sea always lies on the right. 'Continue eastwards' is the most repeated directive, but even this can have odd local quirks. Everyone talks of the east end and the west end of Kirkcaldy High Street, but a glance at the maps shows it runs due north-south! Changes will go on happening too, and any note of these would be welcomed by the author. (Send such addressed to the publishers and marked 'Please forward'.)

The praiseworthy official Fife Coastal Path has been completed from the Forth Road Bridge to St Andrews, and on through to the Tay Road Bridge. The Fife Coastal Path (FCP) is just that, a pedestrian link along the coast. It does not necessarily indicate what to see and do along the way, especially in the towns, so I don't hesitate to deviate; with this guide we are *exploring* the Fife coast not just scurrying along a path. The panorama from the Binn, the interest of the Kirkcaldy Museum and Art Gallery, the mining tunnels at St Andrews Castle, the charm of the East Neuk villages–these just have to be explored. The Fife coast is far too interesting to be rushed through. Comfortable tourist accommodation is plentiful. Public transport is adequate. Make use of everything and weave your own cloth of gold.

The importance of Fife historically is seen in most of the coastal towns being Royal Burghs: Inverkeithing, Kinghorn and Crail as early as the twelfth century, Burntisland, Dysart, Pittenweem and Anstruther in the sixteenth century, Kirkcaldy and St Andrews in the next century, though they are now the biggest towns on the coast. One result of this background is the surviving architectural and historical richness: castles, churches, tolbooths, harbours, doocots, milestones and red-roofed 'little houses'. Every town seemed to have a harbour, ferries abounded and Fife was criss-crossed with routes taking pilgrims to St Andrews, courtiers to the one-time capital of Dunfermline or Falkland (the Stewarts' Balmoral) or merchants to the mines of Culross and the wheatlands of Cupar, or royal corpses to Inchcolm, which followed Iona as the burial place of kings. The Forth and Tay also gave Fife a natural unity if not insularity. Fife was not easily invaded, with the 'lowest bridging points' being Stirling or Perth. Even the Romans hardly touched

Fife. (But you can read later why I live next to Cromwell Road.)

If intending to walk through the route described, or even explore bit by bit, it would pay quickly to skim through one day by car and obtain lots of those fascinating guides that are only available locally. My larger book *The Fife Coast* (Mainstream) has an extensive bibliography and a glossary of architectural features and Scots words that may puzzle (Dae ye ken whit's a loupin-on stane? Wid ye be feart tae meet me up a close or oot in the glebe?) Locals are always happy to chat to visitors– even if you may only pick up the odd word of what Gavin Maxwell once called 'the difficult dialect of Fife'.

That original coast book of mine is more comprehensive and a bit bulky for a pocket, so, with the growing numbers exploring afoot, a more user-friendly guide was called for. While the fuller site descriptions remain valid, the Path itself has seen an incredible number of changes, from the initiating of an official route to the not always helpful construction of golf courses, landslips and housing schemes. My *25 Walks, Fife* (Mercat Press) has also been revised and contains some coastal descriptions.

There are still some sorry sights/sites along the way, more now from personal vandalism than the industrial past (the Fife authorities have had international recognition for their 'green' efforts) and one of the best defences against such misuse is the presence of people. Walkers can be a useful deterrent to vandalism and I feel, too, as things improve, there is less inclination to damage. Late, late, too, we are beginning to realise the sea is not a sewer or rubbish dump, but it will take generations yet to undo the damage from dumping Frances or Randolph colliery redd (spoil) into the Forth. The estuary still sees something like 7000 ship movements a year. The walk gives quite a mix of rural peace and town bustle.

A few more practical points. Heights on the map are given in metres and I see no sense in converting these any longer. Distances are given in miles. As grid squares are 1km across it is hardly difficult to calculate kilometres (8km = 5 miles is a useful guide), and a yard and a metre are close enough for smaller measurements. There are plenty of official signposts at stations and in the towns indicating the FCP and also along its length, but beware, naughty boys enjoy twisting the arms to point in the wrong direction, some may be broken or missing and, of course, we frequently take our own way rather than always following the FCP. But it is our route for much of the way, and as such doesn't need mentioned at every signpost or waymark. Carry and use the maps. A stick is no bad option either; in summer parts can be crowded with unfriendly brambles, blackthorn or nettles. And don't confuse cycleway signs and FCP ones; they can differ.

The word *road* always implies a tarred surface and public use, *track* will be unsurfaced but motorable and may or may not be private for vehicles while quite walkable, *path* means a route only practical on foot. Most of what is described will be right-of-way or a created route, but there may be places which are technically private. If behaviour is sensible there should be no problems. 'Walk softly, take nothing but photographs, leave nothing but memories.' Remember too, we share the land with other users. (I've heard of walkers complaining because there were sheep on the path!) Savour the sea too. Paddle. Swim. Feel the flukies under your toes or find butterfish below the seaweeds. Collect buckies for supper. Walk the vast sands. Watch the abundant bird life. Enjoy pub chat and a haggis supper, B&B and gourmet dining. Make it a fun walk.

Many of the towns are popular summer resorts and there are advantages in going in spring or autumn. Sharp winter days can be good but some attractions will not be open. July and August may still give richer rewards than the 3M flaws of the Highlands: mobs, midges and monsoon. Rainfall on the coast is fairly slight but it can be cold, especially if an east wind is coming from Russia without much love.

The tides will make or mar some sections, so become aware of their movement from the start. Tide tables, set to Leith, are available but it is largely a matter of using one's eyes. Burntisland tides, where I live, are the same as Leith, while Inverkeithing is Leith +9 minutes, Methil —9, Elie —17 and Fife Ness —21. If warnings are needed they will be given in the text, and there are few if any problems an hour or two either side of high tide, so don't over-react to this problem.

Wild camping is virtually impossible (no drinking water) and there are few campsites on the route.

The route is given as a 7-day walk, but most people would want to take longer if looking at all the interests along the way, and at least a day would be needed to explore St Andrews. With reasonable transport, moving about the coast is easy, so a wide range of accommodation opens up. One could use a B&B for several days in a row even. It is perhaps safest to book accommodation ahead day by day. It is a great relief to know the bed for the night is secure. If phoning a B&B, obtain directions of how to find it. Lastly, if the British Open Golf Championship is being played at St Andrews, every bed in the East Neuk will be taken and the St Cuthbert's Way would be a better option. On several occasions the route edges golf courses and it is only courteous not to disturb play. Stand still and watch (which sometimes causes *more* nervousness!) and keep dogs in control (players don't really want golf balls 'fetched') but, quite seriously, watch out for flying golf balls. (The Golf Museum in St Andrews has a stuffed skylark in a glass case, along with the ball that killed it.)

While every care has been taken to describe the route accurately, neither author nor publisher accepts responsibility regarding information, or its interpretation by readers. Signposts vanish (or are turned round!), brambles grow, paths vanish under new roads or housing schemes. Before many years I'm sure there will be plenty alterations. As many are improvements, I hope so. While welcoming information on changes, entering into correspondence on such matters is not possible. There should always be an expectation of the unexpected on any walk. We explore and walk the Fife coast for fun.

The Fife Coastal Path was opened in June 2003, but several local problems remain (and may never be completely overcome) between Fife Ness and St Andrews, largely due to landslips and, of course, the tide. Golf course construction is likely to continue between the St Andrews Bay development and Kinkell Braes caravan park. So great care should be taken if continuing along this coast.

Hamish Brown
Burntisland 2004

PRACTICAL INFORMATION

Opening hours have a habit of changing and it does no harm to telephone ahead to avoid disappointment. Tourist Information Offices can usually provide times if the place itself is closed.

Tourist Information Offices

Dundee, 21 Castle St., DD1 3AA. Tel: 01382-527527.

Forth Road Bridge, Queensferry Lodge Hotel, N. Queensferry KY11 1HP. Tel: 01383-417759.

Kirkcaldy, 19 Whytecauseway, KY1 1XF. Tel: 01592-267775.

St Andrews, 70 Market Street, KY16 9NU. Tel: 01334-472021.

Edinburgh, 3 Princes Street, EH2 20P. Tel: 0131-473-3800.

Anstruther, Scottish Fisheries Museum, KY10 3BA. Tel: 01333-311073. (Apr-Sept.)

Crail, Crail Museum and Heritage Centre, 62-64 Marketgate, KY10 3TL. Tel: 01333-450869. (Apr-Sept.)

Transport

Public Transport Information Line: available weekday office hours. Tel: 01592-416060.

Rail enquiries: Tel: 08457-484950.

Traveline Scotland: 08.00-20.00 daily. Tel: 08706-082608.

Local Stagecoach: Tel: 01592-642394.

Taxis: often a forgotten option and readily available in the coast towns and villages.

Tide Times: Fife Ports: (Methil docks). Tel: 01333-426725.

Maps: OS Landranger 1:50,000. Nos 59, 65, 66. Explorer 1:25,000. Nos 350, 367, 371.

Sites and Services, Opening Hours, etc.

Aberdour Castle. Tel: 01383-860519. Open: Apr-Sept 09.30-18.30; Oct-Mar, Mon-Wed, Sat 09.30-16.30, Thur mornings, Sun afternoon. (Historic Scotland.)

Adam Smith Centre (see Kirkcaldy)

Anstruther, Scottish Fisheries Museum. Tel: 01333-310628. Open: Apr-Oct. Weekdays 10.00-17.30. Sun 11.00-17.00. Winter 10.00-16.30 and 14.00-16.30.

British Golf Museum (see St Andrews)

Buckhaven Museum, College Street (library building). Tel: 01592-412860. Open: library hours.

Burntisland (Beacon Leisure Centre–swimming pool). Tel: 01592-872211. Open: Mon-Fri 08.00-21.30, weekends: 08.00-20.00.

Burntisland Church. Tel: 01592-873275 (Custodian/curator). (Details also on church entrance notice board)

Burntisland Edwardian Fair Museum, Library Building, 102 High Street. Tel: 01592-412860. Open: library hours (mornings only).

Byre Theatre (see St Andrews)

Cambo Gardens, Kingsbarns. Tel: 01333-450054. Open: All year 10.00-dusk.

Crail Museum and Heritage Centre, Marketgate. Tel: 01333-450869. Open: Easter-spring weekends 14.00-17.00. June-Sept 10.00-17.00, Sun 14.00-17.00.

Crail Pottery. Tel: 01333-451212. Open: All year, 08.00-17.00. Weekends 10.00-17.00.

Crawford Art Centre (see St Andrews)

Deep Sea World (see North Queensferry)

Dysart, John McDouall Stuart Museum. Tel: 01592-412860. Open: June-Aug daily 14.00-17.00.

East Sands Leisure Complex (see St Andrews)

Forth Bridges Exhibition, Queensferry Lodge Hotel. Tel: 0131-225-6741. Open: Daily, all year, 09.00-21.00.

Inchcolm Abbey. Tel: 01383-823332. Open: Easter—Sept 09.30-18.30. (Historic Scotland) (Ferry: see *Maid of the Forth*)

Inverkeithing Museum. Tel: 01383-313595. Open: All year, Thur-Sun 12.00-14.00.

Kellie Castle and Garden. Tel: 01333-720271. Open: Easter, May-Sept and Oct weekends 13.30-17.30. Gardens, all year 09.30-dusk. (NTS)

Kirkcaldy, Adam Smith Theatre. Tel: 01592-412929. Open: All year. Café.

Kirkcaldy Museum and Art Gallery. Tel: 01592-412860. Open: Mon-Sat 10.30-17.00. Sun 14.00-17.00. (Café)

Kirkcaldy Swimming Pool. Tel: 01592-412655. Open: Mon, Fri 08.00-18.00, Tues-Thurs 08.00-19.45, weekends 08.00-16.00. (Café)

Letham Glen. Open all year.

Levenmouth Pool and Sports Centre. Tel: 01333-592500. Open: Mon-Fri 08.00-22.00, weekends 08.00-21.00. (Café)

Maid of the Forth. (Inchcolm ferry), Hawes Pier, Queensferry. Tel: 0131-331 4857. (Summary of sailings in text)

May Island sailings (*May Princess*) Tel: 01333-310103. May-Oct.

Methil Heritage Centre (The Museum of Levenmouth) Tel: 01333-422100. Open: Tues-Thur 11.00-16.30, Sat 13.00-16.30.

North Queensferry: Deep Sea World. Tel: 01383-411880. Open: generally, 10.00-18.00 summer, 11.00-17.00 winter.

Pittenweem, St Fillan's Cave. Open: All year, Mon-Sat 09.00-17.30. Winter, closed Mon. Key: at Gingerbread Horse Craft and Coffee Shop, 9 High St.

Queensferry Museum. Tel: 0131-3315545. Open: All year, Mon, Thur-Sat 10.00-17.00 (shut 13.00-14.15), Sun 12.00-17.00.

Ravenscraig Castle. Open all year. (No custodian; parts locked)

Silverburn Estate, Leven. (Garden/woodland walks) Tel: 01333-427568. Open all year.

St Andrews Aquarium. Tel: 01334-474786. Open: Daily from 10.00.

St Andrews, Botanic Gardens, Cannongate. Tel: 01334-460046. Open: All year, 7 days 10.00-19.00. (Oct-Apr 10.00—16.00)

St Andrews, British Golf Museum. Tel: 01334-460046. Open: Easter-Oct 09.30-17.30. Winter 11.00-15.00 (closed Tues/Wed)

St Andrews, Byre Theatre, 36 South Street. Tel: 01334-476288.

St Andrews Castle and Visitor Centre. Tel: 01334-477196. Open: Apr-Sept 09.30-18.30, Oct-Mar 09.30-16.30. (Sun 14.00-16.30) (Historic Scotland)

St Andrews Cathedral and Museum. Tel: 01334-472563. Open: Apr-Sept 09.30-18.30, Oct-Mar 09.30-16.30. (Sun 14.00-16.30) (Historic Scotland)

St Andrews, Crawford Arts Centre, 93 North Street. Tel: 01334-474610. Open: Mon-Sat 10.00-17.00, Sun 14.00-17.00.

St Andrews East Sands Leisure Centre. Tel: 01334-476506. Open: 09.00-22.00.

St Andrews Museum, Kinburn Park. Tel: 01334-412690. Open: Apr-Sept 10.00-17.00, Oct-Mar, Mon-Fri 10.30-16.00, weekends 12.30-17.00.

St Andrews Preservation Trust Museum and Garden, 12 North Street. Tel: 01334-477629. Open 14.00-17.00, June-Sept and other odd times.

St Fillan's Cave (see Pittenweem)

St Monans Windmill. Interior open July/August 11.00-16.00.

Scottish Fisheries Museum (see Anstruther)

Bookshops

Ottakars, High Street, Kirkcaldy. Tel: 01592-263755.

John Smith, Market Street, St Andrews. Tel: 01334-475122.

East Neuk Books, Rodger Street, Anstruther. Tel: 01333-310474.

Further Reading

There is a wealth of local booklets only found in Tourist Offices and local outlets while libraries along the way have extensive collections. For the architecture, J. Gifford, *Fife* (Penguin) is authoritative and entertaining. A bird and/or flower guide may be worth carrying. As mentioned, my *The Fife Coast* (Mainstream) has a comprehensive bibliography and a glossary of Scots words and architectural terms.

COAST AND COUNTRY CODE

Before leaving home:

- Acquire adequate waterproofs, comfortable boots and emergency items.
- If going alone, organise some system of phoning home or to someone acting as base. If you break a leg by the Kenly Water it is nice to know someone will be worried sooner rather than later and send out an SOS on your behalf. Know the distress signal: six flashes, shouts, whistle blasts per minute.
- Learn something of elementary first-aid and prepare a small field kit.

Plan within your capabilities. Tired people are far more accident-prone.

Read up about the areas being visited. The curious traveller is usually the happiest traveller. Buy all the maps you need and prepare by reading through this book *with* the maps.

During the walk:

- Close all gates. There is nothing calculated to annoy farmers more than having to round up strayed livestock. Don't go over walls or through fences or hedges—there are few places without gates or stiles on our route.
- Leave livestock, crops and machinery alone.
- Guard against all risk of fires.
- Dump your litter in bins, not on the shore or in the countryside. You'll see some bad sights, so don't add to them. Polythene bags can mean disaster to a grazing cow, broken glass is wicked for both man and beast, and drink cans are an insufferable eyesore.
- Leave wildlife alone. Collecting eggs or flowers is illegal. 'Lost' creatures are rare; parents will soon find their young unless some unhelpful person has carried them off.

- Walk quietly in the countryside. Nature goes unobtrusively and you'll see far more if you are not clad in garish colours and walking with a ghetto-blaster.
- While most of this trip is on rights-of-way or other established walking routes, it is still running through a farmed and used landscape, so treat it with respect. Local people's livelihood depends on this countryside. There is no wilderness.
- Dogs are best left at home. In sheep/farming country they need strict control so neither dog nor owner can relax much. In the lambing season (February-May) dogs are particularly unwelcome.
- Be extra careful when walking on roads, however quiet these appear. Maniac drivers are no respecters of pedestrians.
- Keep an eye on incoming tides. Do not pick up unusual or mystery objects from the beach. Report them to the police.
- Swimming may be dangerous and is best kept for recognised beaches. It is unwise to swim alone.
- Make local contacts. Rural people are still sociable and a 'crack' will often be welcomed. Use the tourist offices and bookshops along the way to widen knowledge and enrich your experience. Those met in bars, cafés or overnight stops are often a fund of information. They may even find *us* interesting.

It is rewarding to keep a record of some kind, one's own notes and photographs, perhaps with added postcards, drawings, anything that appeals. In later years a record like this becomes a treasured souvenir.

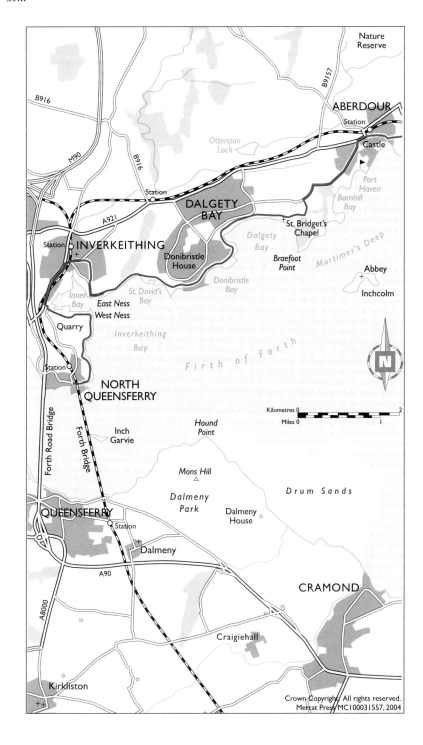

I

Into Fife: Queensferry, Forth Bridge, Inverkeithing

O.S. 65

'Out of the world and into Fife' may have been true centuries ago and the mind can speculate on how those taking the Queen's Ferry in ancient times would react to seeing the bridges that span the firth today. The railway bridge is simply one of the most recognisable and remarkable bridges in the world and the road bridge is a graceful enough way 'out of the world and into Fife'.

In practical terms the easiest way to start is to take the train from Edinburgh or Fife to **Dalmeny Station** which perches high above Queensferry at the south end of the great bridge. Even if using a car, parking at or near the station is a good option; you may well be catching a train back to the vehicle. Bus no. 43 runs from central Edinburgh (Waterloo Place, Charlotte Square), every 20 minutes.

Leaving Dalmeny Station, turn right on descending the ramp to reach a roundabout. From the bus stop opposite take the path up and along by the railway. This then runs down and swings right by a bridge over an abandoned line before passing under one of the approach arches of the Forth Bridge. Turn left to descend the 120 steps of Jacob's Ladder to reach **Queensferry**, the trellised girders of the bridge high overhead. The town is Queensferry or just The Ferry, not South Queensferry. (On the Fife shore is the old North Ferry now called North Queensferry.)

The Hawes Inn appears at the start of Robert Louis Stevenson's story *Kidnapped* and also appears in Scott's *Antiquary*. RLS often walked these shores, watched the ships, went canoeing and enjoyed, in his own words, 'one unbroken round of pleasure and suspense'. His very ill health led him to live life the more fully. 'I have but to see the words snell, flae, gurly, and scouthering and I think again that I can hear the great wind that comes tearing over the Forth from Burntisland and the northern hills. I can hear it howl in the chimney and if I turn my face northwards I feel its icy kisses on my cheek.'

Workers on the Railway Bridge

Opposite the Hawes Inn is the lifeboat station and Hawes Pier, designed by John Rennie and, till the road bridge was built, the pier used for the vehicular ferry across the Forth to Fife. The light at the end of the pier has its partner on the Fife pier.

The Railway Bridge towers above us, still one of the most visually stunning bridges ever built. When constructed, sailing ships would be passing below its cantilevered spans. Originally work had started to a design by Sir Thomas Bouch, but when his Tay Bridge blew down in 1879 with the loss of 75 lives parliament cancelled the project. The 'floating railway' ferry from Burntisland which the bridge would replace had been his very successful brainchild.

Benjamin Baker designed the present masterpiece with William Arrol the contractor. Baker's career began as an apprentice in a South Wales ironworks, and he had worked on Victoria Station in London, was a partner with John Fowler in creating the city's underground system and helped bring Cleopatra's Needle from Egypt to the Thames embankment. Workaholic Arrol had already built bridges over the Wear, Thames and Nile. Fowler took the first railway over the Thames (Pimlico Bridge) and built St Enoch's station in Glasgow. Baker became his assist-ant, then partner and finally took on the Forth Bridge responsibility.

Up to 5000 men took seven years to built the bridge, the first to use steel throughout and, at the time, the biggest-ever man-made structure. Not everyone admired the bridge. John Ruskin loathed it and one book thought it crude and suggested towers and finials be added and gilt paint be applied to its length.

One of the few examples of big being beautiful, the bridge has impressive material statistics: 54,160 tons of steel, 740,000 cubic feet of granite, 48,400 of other stone, 64,300 of concrete, 21,000 tons of cement and 6½ million rivets. There is an area of 145 acres to paint regularly, taking a team of 20 about 4-6 years and 17 tons/7000 gallons of paint. Thatcherite savings saw rapid deterio-ration, so remedial work has kept the bridge under wraps for some years now. The notion of starting at one end and working to the other, over and over again, is a myth but the work is exacting, the worker often literally hang-ing on with one hand and painting with the other. During construction Baker saw a hole pierced through a four-inch timber by a dropped spanner. Throwing lucky pennies out of the train is not a good idea. One worker escaped injury dramatically when a spanner, falling 100 metres, went down inside his waistcoat and out of his trousers.

The three cantilever towers stand on platforms called caissons: 400 ton, 70 ft. diameter wrought-iron cylinders which were constructed at Queensferry and floated out. On site, concrete was poured into them till they sank to the bottom. A 7 ft. space was left at the bottom, kept dry by compressed air, and the workers cut away the seabed below their feet to reach the final sturdy base. This area was then filled with concrete too and steel bedplates affixed to the top so the work on the superstructure could start. (On the Road Bridge the sheer weight of the south tower caisson sank it through the boulder clay of the riverbed.) The three towers worked up and outwards till the spreading arms met. On a hot summer day the bridge can expand by 8 feet. The bridge is $1^5/8$ miles long and reaches 361 feet above high water level. Two tracks cross it, and such is its strength that it copes still with 200 modern trains a day crossing at speeds up to 50 m.p.h. Edward VII, as Prince of Wales, opened the bridge in 1890. It cost £3 million. Fife's current logo portrays the Forth Bridge. Though not it does not appear in John Buchan's book, two films of *The 39 Steps* couldn't resist setting an episode on the bridge.

The lost of life was small for the period: 57. Baker lost no men under the sea, for instance, yet 119 of 600 employed on the Brooklyn Bridge had the bends, 16 fatally, while a caisson in St Petersburg sank onto 28 men with fatal results. Look well then at the masterpiece of masterpieces.

Maid of the Forth (Inchcolm Ferry) is based on Hawes pier and operates various cruises but of these, very much worthwhile for its Fife connections, is a visit to Inchcolm Abbey (see Appendix 1). This runs at weekends in April-June and early October. During July-September there are daily sailings and, at weekends, passengers are also picked up at North Queensferry. Check details in advance. Seals and dolphins are seen regularly. East of the bridge lies the oil tanker terminal of Hound Point where tankers can load a million gallons of Grangemouth-refined oil in 24 hours. The three tugs based there are also equipped for fire-fighting and dealing with an oil spillage. The Forth has mercifully been spared any disasters like the Alaska mess when *Exxon Valdez* went aground. Incidentally, she calls here still–but has been given another name. The QE2 has used the Hound Point terminal and crew boats use Hawes Pier.

Set back, beyond the Hawes Inn, is the large brick

Bridge House which was office and staff quarters for the bridgebuilders, then a sailors' home and now flats. **Queensferry** has been declared an 'Outstanding Conservation Area' and is worth exploring on the way through, however briefly. There's a reproduction Victorian pillar box on the promenade as we head west–and did you see the seals on the road by Hawes Pier?

The burry man

Seals Craig Hotel is the site of the old East Port (town gateway) and starts the picturesque High Street which has buildings dating to the sixteenth century, some terraced on top of others, like Chester's Rows, or separated by 'closes'. The museum (seaward side) will explain much of what we see and some things we don't such as the shale oil industry which honeycombs Lothian and Fife and under the Forth between. Note the figure of the 'burry man', a now unique ancient custom that is still observed (second Friday in August) when a man proceeds round the town with floral staffs and clothed from ankles to crown in burdock burrs.

East Terrace ends at Black Castle, so painted and dated 1626 with the marriage lintel of William Lowrie and Marion Speedie. Lowrie was a skipper and when he and his crew were lost at sea two local women were accused of causing the disaster and burnt as witches. (At least eight women were burnt in the 1643-44 period, the minister being a bit of a fanatic.) Tortures, like sleep deprivation, were applied–sounds quite modern. A secret stair goes up in the thickness of the Black Castle walls.

Beside Black Castle the Vennel runs up to the 1633 Auld Kirk (now a house) which has a graveyard with some interesting stones, one of a ship under sail, one with navigational instruments and there are other trades shown too–besides a great variety of skulls! One wall has the holes (bee-boles) where skeps of bees were kept. The church bell, dated 1635, is inscribed 'Cursed be they that takes it' which may have something to do with its survival. A key for the graveyard can be obtained from the council offices in the museum building (during office hours).

The Ferry Tap next to the Vennel has dates 1674 and 1683. Steps lead up to Mid Terrace and, halfway along, look into Hamilton's Close. There's a gap, then West Terrace. Continuing, there are a couple more old hostelries, The Staghorn Hotel name recalls a stage coach killing a stray stag at the time the inn was being built. The Queensferry Arms sign shows just that though the royal burgh has a second coat of arms showing Queen Margaret aboard a ferry. This area is dominated by the old tolbooth (customs and tax office, court and prison, burgh chambers, weights and measures office etc) but the mercat cross was removed in 1764 due to increased road traffic. The clock on the tower commemorates Queen Victoria's Jubilee and the Rosebery Hall was gifted by the fifth earl in 1894 (Dalmeny, their estates, lie east of the town). Wells and war memorial are found here too.

The Loan, left at the busy junction, is the town's main approach road. Across it is Plewlands House, given to the NTS in 1955 and restored as flats. The motto translates 'Christ is my hope' and the initials are of Samuel Wilson and Anna Poulton. Facing the Loan is a square which became the local market place on the western boundary of the burgh. See if you can spot the stone with an owl perched on a bell, dated 1879. Covenanter Lane commemorates Donald Cargill and Henry Hall, wanted Covenanters, escaping after a fight in the inn here in 1680. Hall later died at the hands of Dalyell of the Binns and Cargill was executed in the capital.

Walk down Harbour Lane. Hugh Baird (of Union Canal fame) rebuilt the harbour in 1817. Ferries used whichever slip was best for prevailing conditions: here, Sealscraig, Port Neuk and, later, Hawes Pier. It was once crowded with fishing boats. Coal, potatoes and stone were shipped out and grain brought in for the distillery. Head west by the picnic tables and round to the main road again, with the Friary buildings to the left, which date back to 1330 and had a chequered history before being part restored in 1890 as an Episcopal church, which it still is.

Turn right along the main road past the police station to a junction. The right fork (not ours) leads under the Road Bridge to Port Edgar, named after the Saxon prince, brother of Margaret, who was chased out of England by William the Conqueror (*1066 and All That*). Margaret became Queen of Scotland and had the ferry named after her. Port Edgar is now a vast marina. We take the left fork (signposted for Linlithgow, Bo'ness) which leads up to the other Forth Bridge.

If the railway bridge did not exist the 1½ mile **Forth Road Bridge** would enjoy greater fame I'm sure. When built, it was the largest suspension bridge in Europe and the fourth largest in the world. The central span is 3,300

Forth Road Bridge

ft. long with 1,340 ft. side spans, a southern approach of 1,437 ft. and a northern of 842 ft. and deep cuttings. The cables were made of 12,000 galvanised steel wires, each able to bear 100 tons; 314 wires made one strand and 37 strands one cable. The towers reach 512 feet. In all, 39,000 tons of steel and 150,000 cubic feet of concrete were used. Cost: £19.5 million (and 7 lives). And now there are calls for a second bridge. Fifteen million vehicles cross the bridge each year. Its historic and aesthetic status has led to the bridge receiving 'Listed' status.

The earliest record of a crossing here is documented at the time Queen Margaret died. This refugee princess married Malcolm Canmore and was an early commuter between Dunfermline and Edinburgh. The crossing became the Queen's Ferry, as did the town on the Lothian side. The Fife landing was just North Ferry till last century. Storms and strong currents could make crossings hazardous, as Alexanders I and III were to find, and Charles II was to complain at the tolls. The opening of the bridge by the Queen in 1964 brought an end to 800 years of ferry use, which was frustrating latterly with nearly a million vehicles a year crossing, but it was fascinating to watch the construction from the ferry queue over 7 years.

Walk up to go under the bridge by a cycle lane but then turn left to go under it again and on up to use the eastern walkway. Up-river views are backed by the Ochils, but for those heading along the Fife coast the east side is the natural choice. The River Forth rises on the slopes of Ben Lomond and twists and turns for a hundred miles to reach here. On a windy day the bridge seems to sway. In fact, it does, by intent, anything up to 22 feet in big gales. (Motorists seldom notice anything then, except a speed restriction.) One construction worker survived falling 180 feet into the sea. Fatalities since have been from road accidents, or suicide jumps (not publicised to discourage copycat attempts). One mystery remains. After blasting, a shaft at the south end was closed for six weeks, and when re-opened a dead sailor was found inside. The bridge has the lighting, drainage, surfacing, maintenance and financial complexities of a small town, and work, as on the Rail Bridge, never stops.

At the Fife end of the bridge on the Ferry Hills pedestrian steps lead down for North Queensferry, but before doing so pass under the bridge and up on the west side where there are several points of interest, including a viewing platform, a model showing the cantilever system of the Rail Bridge, a tourist information office, Bridges Exhibition, shop, hotel, café and restaurant.

When the steps down from the Road Bridge reach the main road be very careful about crossing. Cars come down round the blind corner at speed. Turn off beside the **North Queensferry** town sign onto a footpath and steps down to a housing area. The path runs between back gardens, then turns right onto Ferry Barns Court (no name visible to start with). Turn left down to the T-junction. Note the anchorage for the bridge cables off to the right.

Turn left up the road, passing the entrance to the marina which is based on the old ferry slip, and reach the main road again. Turn right to walk on into the village which is dominated by the Railway Bridge, the rhythm of passing trains its heartbeat. Opposite the house with a 1771 lintel date go down the right hand steps to Willie's Well and follow round the bay on the King's Way–once the royal commuting route to Dunfermline.

This leads out to the Ferrybridge Inn on Main Street. Turn right. Note attractive Post Office Lane on the left. Facing the Albert Hotel the date 1693 is on what was the Black Cat Inn. Thomas Peastie and Bessie Craich have their initials above a window. (Genealogists in Scotland are given a help by lintels and gravestones always giving the wife's original surname.) Next to the Albert Hotel is a rather good 1990 gap-site building. At the slip turning area is a hexagonal building with a domed light and a flue indicating the light was originally oil-fired. The last, castellated house above the slip was once the ferry offices, called Mount Hooly, an obsolete word for canny or slow, which is how the masons worked! The officials sat at an octagonal table so no one person had precedence. Notices at the slip give details of sailings to Inchcolm (see Appendix 1). Victoria and Albert landed at the Town Pier in 1842, hence the hotel name. Behind it is the Cadgers' Slip where the cadgers (carters) met the fishing boats.

Walk back and turn right past the hotel and follow Battery Road round till you are below the bridge–Meccano writ large–beside one of its great towers. Terns may be diving in summer and seals are often spotted from the viewing point. The island straddled by the bridge is Inchgarvie, still bristling with old defences. When the Picts defeated the Angles at the Battle of Athelstaneford the Anglian king's head was stuck up on a spear on the island as a warning not to cross the Forth. Burntisland, Inchgarvie and Rosyth were forts which were a thorn in the flesh to Cromwell, but eventually he won a battle at Inverkeithing and Scotland fell to his rule. Ironically, his mother was a Rosyth Stuart.

Head back but take a path to the right signed 'Chapel Place leading to Helen Place'. The 600-year-old chapel dedicated to the patron saint of travellers is on the left, access locked to prevent vandalism. Many sailors and ferrymen are buried in the cemetery and they added the wall round the site as a plaque indicates. 'This is done by sailers in North Ferrie 1752'. One stone inside is inscribed, 'Now here we lay at anchor/ With many of our fleet/ In hopes to weigh at the last day/ Our Admiral Christ to meet.'

Narrow Helen Place still has an old open drain. The cottage at the end, village school till 1827, was called the Malinkie. Turn right at the Malinkie gable and right again if going down to visit the Deep Sea World, one of Fife's most popular attractions. If just continuing turn left at the Malinkie and then left again to walk up Post Office Lane.

Deep Sea World was set up in 1993 to make use of the old Battery Quarry which provided the million-gallon aquarium 'tank' through which visitors travel to see the wonders of the deep. There are exhibitions, and audio-visual presentations, facilities for education use and a large café. The Battery Quarry opened in 1764 and its whinstone was used in the bridge's foundations, the Forth and Clyde Canal, Leith Docks, London streets, and exported to the Low Countries and even Russia. Sea water flooding stopped production in 1924. The Battery itself was set up on the crags above following the raid on the Forth by John Paul Jones in 1799. Barrage balloons and guns successfully spoiled raids through both World Wars. Hitler was so depressed at the failure he had pictures faked to show the bridge had been hit.

If returning from Deep Sea World backtrack to the Post Office Lane and from it turn right to the crossroads with a break ahead and a cluster of wells and the signposting

In the bay, Port Laing

for the start of the **Fife Coastal Path** (FCP). Most obvious is the 1816 Waterloo monument in the shape of a Napoleon's hat. A standard Victorian well stands above, painted black, then there is a plaque on another closed well which shows Europa and the Bull and what looks like a village lassie having a stushie with a foreign sailor—as no doubt occurred at a busy well. (Up the steep brae there's a Jubilee Well–and note the outside stairs on the houses on the left.)

The path rises to pass under the railway and round Carlingnose Point, a SWT Wildlife Reserve, with splendid views to the bridge above St James' Harbour which is now a classy housing estate (spot the old lighthouse!), and out to the estuary and Hound Point tanker terminal. The *Witch's Nose* has uncommon flowers like bloody cranesbill, field gentian and dropwort. Fulmars have taken to nesting here and in other places along our walk. At the far end of the big quarry site briefly divert right to the cliff edge for the best viewpoint. There's a derelict section of pier below. The route drops to a small road which leads to the bay of Port Laing.

Port Laing is a small, grey, sandy bay tucked in under Carlingnose, whose heights once held batteries with barracks on the bay. There's a duelling stone marking where a Captain Gurley was killed in 1824 by a Mr Westall after they'd squabbled over a gambling debt. The latter had to flee the country.

A track wends up to reach North Queensferry station but we continue on past three smart houses which have spilled down onto the bay itself. From the far end of the bay the path weaves on through to pick up another small access road. The view to the estuary opens out and the white 'clean-gleaming' houses of St David's Harbour stand out. The Inverkeithing inlet remains hidden for a while, though the piers, old and new, on the other side look so near. Round a bend–and all is revealed. Oddly the two arms of the inlet are called East Ness and West Ness though they lie north and south of each other.

We are directed aside from the quarry: **Cruicks Quarry**, which is the only one locally still operating. Begun in 1828, its stone still goes all over Britain and abroad. Most recently barges took stone for strengthening the sea defences at Dysart, the Wemyss villages and the railway embankment above Pettycur sands. The scale doesn't really show from here but the small road to North Queensferry from Inverkeithing (Ferryhills Road) has a viewing platform. The central hole goes far below sea level. Pennant on his travels noted quarrying in this area in the nineteenth century. Only the quarry names survive now: Ferry Toll, Welldean, Lucknow, Jubilee, Battery etc. At the start of this century a quarryman, working a 10-hour day, earned £1 for his labours. The quarry is one of the few industrial spots on our coastal route.

The cranes and piles of scrap mark what was once Ward's shipbreaking yard. I can recall a huge carrier, the *Implacable*, being cannibalised in 1955 and the proud *Mauritania* in 1965. The hall of the office building was decorated with the name-plates of scores more: *Revenge, Royal Sovereign, Rodney, Majestic*. This last was actually German in origin but was a trophy of World War I. Changed from *Bismarck* to *Majestic* (sounds like a hotel!), she was once the largest liner operating. There was over-capacity following the Cunard/White Star merger and *Majestic* was delivered here for scrapping. However, with Hitler's war looming, the Royal Navy took her as a training ship, renamed HMS *Caledonia* and based at Rosyth. There was something of a panic when the war began and she was beached, went on fire and so ended in Ward's after all. It took several years to dismantle the ship. Now scrap has replaced shipbreaking. Industry constantly changes, for we've just walked along a one-time railway to Cruickness, the piers all decay with transport changes, and gone completely are the salt-pans, woodyard, lime-kiln and bonemill. On the left, well hidden, lies the Jamestown Pond–a sanctuary for the azure damsel fly.

Continue under the railway to turn right at the main road. Walking on we pass an Episcopal church which looks like an alpine chapel, a B&B (with elephant gates) which calls itself Niravaana, some allotments, St Peter in Chains church, Scout hall and then a more imposing front with a date, MDCCCXXXIII, which challenges interpretation. **Inverkeithing** is a very old town with some surviving buildings worth seeing.

Off right is the friary, now the local museum, in the *hospitium* of a Grey Friars Monastery dating back to the fourteenth century. Behind are gardens in what would have been the cloisters. Continue along the wide High Street, passing the Royal Hotel, birthplace of Samuel Greig. He was born in 1735 and died as Grand Admiral of Russia. A schoolboy trip to the Baltic in his father's trading vessel started off his sea career. He served with Hawke, was at the siege of Havana and volunteered for Russian service. He was largely responsible for destroy-ing the 'invincible' Turkish fleet, then reor-ganised the Baltic fleet for Catherine the Great, beat off Swedish attacks and built the Kronstadt Fort so well (Carling-nose stone) that Napier's British fleet, 85 years later, found it 'a hard nut to crack'. One son also became a Russian admi-ral, two others served in the British navy and an-other was Russian consul in London where he died at the age of 29, and his young widow then married a Dr Somerville, of whom

Mercat Cross, Inverkeithing

An old house in Inverkeithing

more when we explore Burntisland. Another cousin also made it as a Russian admiral–and so too, did Scots-born Yankee John Paul Jones.

Along a bit, the Burgh Arms (dated 1664-1888), has an attractive sign and another door is dated 1688 with I.B's lintel text: 'God's providence is my inheritance'. Then we come to Bank Street and the gem of the burgh's sixteenth-century mercat cross, vividly painted as it would have been in those days. The shields are of Robert III, Queen Annabella Drummond, Duke of Rothesay and the red heart of the Douglas.

Houses built entirely of stone seldom pre-date the end of the fifteenth century (so not much survives from before that period) but the Fife coast is unusually rich in early stone building such as we see here. A forestair leading to upper-level living areas was a common feature and partly defensive (a stair was an effective defence in pre-gunpowder days) and partly practical (below lay traders' cellars, room for fishermen's nets etc). Crowstep gables allowed beams to be laid across to work on thatch or pantiles, often at too steep a pitch for standing on. The pantiles came from the Low Countries as ballast for the ships trading salt and coal from the Fife coast.

Across Townhill Street lies the fine old town hall or tolbooth which also has an outside stair, coat of arms and so on. Debtors were imprisoned on the top floor beside the 1467 bell, a court room occupied the middle floor and the 'black hole' (prison) lay below. The mercat cross would originally have been nearby and luckenbooths (lockable stalls) and market day activity would echo down the streets.

Turn right once up past the tolbooth onto Church Street, as the High Street has become, to reach the church, the tower of which looks, and is, old (fourteenth-century) and the adjacent graveyard with many of the stones sunk deeply in the ground but full of interest. See if you can add to my tally of trade symbols: weaver (shuttle), sailor (anchor), tailor (scissors), butcher (cleaver), wright (compass and square)… The church hall opposite is in the Fordell Lodging which dates to about 1670 and was the 'town house' of the Hendersons of Fordell.

That really does for exploring Inverkeithing. The railway station lies five minutes walk further along past the church and buses all call at the town centre where there are restaurants, cafés, pubs, chip-shops etc. We'll pick up the route again at the tolbooth.

II
From Inverkeithing to Burntisland

O.S. 65, 66

From the Tolbooth head down (Townhall Street) then turn right (Port Street) to descend to a footbridge over a railway. Rather than head off along Preston Crescent opposite, walk along the road to where the Keithing Burn becomes a sea inlet. The Quayside pub and the entrance to the Caldwell's/Inveresk paperworks lie at the road end. Cross a footbridge to the large green open area, Ballast Bank, and follow its seaward edge. Inverkeithing Harbour now only has a few pleasure boats, but at one time a waggonway from Halbeath, near Dunfermline, brought coal down for shipping abroad.

Picking up the coastal path we come on the huge Prestonhill Quarry, the empty heart filled with water, its derelict pier fretworking out to sea. The path leads us on round to St David's Bay. (A path off left goes up through Letham Hill Wood to the recently built Dalgety Bay railway station.) **Dalgety Bay** (the town) was only created in the 1960s but now invades down to St David's Harbour and inland to the A921 coast road by the Donibristle and Hillend industrial estates. The town is identikit building, no more Scottish than Margate. Fortunately we skirt most of its amoebic sprawl.

The harbour at St David's Bay was built in 1752 to export coal from the Fordell mines inland, the coal being brought down along wooden rails, drawn by horses (as at Inverkeithing)–Fife's first 'railway'. Fordell Castle was the home of the late exotic MP, Sir Nicholas Fairbairn. The harbour serviced minesweepers in the war, Donibristle had a naval base and H.M.S. *Cochrane*, while every prominence had its defences because of the Forth Bridge.

The St David's Harbour development is stylish with a touch of the vernacular in red roofs and harling. A curve of bay leads to the development, the path running outside the houses to reach the heart of the 'village', a green facing the remnant of harbour and with a big anchor much loved of children at play. For the next stretch paths and roads alternate as the coastline is followed. The houses enjoy magnificent views up-river and over to Hound Point. At a gap in the housing there is a knoll with mature trees, left, while, right, the FCP breaks off (just before the first house on the seaward side of the road) to dip down into Hopeward Wood. On a crisp February day this proved a rich birding area with all the garden birds, mobs of blackbirds, goldfinch, speugs (sparrows), siskins, greenfinch, a blackcap, a yaffle (green wood-pecker) undulating ahead and a din of shore calls from gulls, crows, eiders, redshanks, curlews and oystercatch-ers. Steps lead up to reach Bathing House Wood, with Downing Point jutting out into the firth and offering the best panorama of the day. Do visit this site, marked with dual WW2 gun emplacements. The point seems to aim straight at Inchcolm with the Bass Rock on the horizon.

Swing down through the wood and keep along the bay with its 'superior housing'. When the way on is blocked, a path detours round the shoreside houses briefly. It is worth making a brief detour out and back through the rook-loud Chapel Wood to see Donibristle chapel. This was completed as an Episcopal chapel in 1732 and is the family vault of the Morays. At least nine earls are thought to be buried within. The twelfth Earl of Mo-ray was reputedly seven foot tall, and the find of an eight-foot coffin seems to confirm this. The west face bears a fine coat of arms.

The seaside is regained to walk along below the old Donibristle House site, now restored as luxury flats and with the magnificent old iron entrance gateway setting off the balanced splendour.

Donibristle House has had a chequered history. Its first mention is in the twelfth century, when it was the resi-dence of the Abbot of Inchcolm. An Earl of Moray was the illegitimate son of James V and so half-brother to Mary Queen of Scots, but best known is his grandson, the Bonnie Earl o' Moray of the song. After he fell foul of James VI, the Earl of Huntly and his cronies fired the house and murdered those escaping. (The murdered earl's son was later to marry the murderer's daughter!) That fire was in 1592. In 1790 the west wing of a new

Donibristle House

house went up in flames, and in 1858 the main house burnt down. In 1912 the shell was pulled down leaving the two wings. An underground passage linked them with cellars and kitchens so spacious they could garage several double decker buses. The west wing went on fire in 1985. The site was used by the navy in the war, was later the estate office and is now the heart of the luxury housing development. I hope they have adequate fire insurance.

We round to come in sight of another small harbour. Here Robert Moffat, the famous missionary and father-in-law of David Livingstone, nearly lost his life when pulling a fellow worker from the sea. He was then working in the gardens of the big house. Overlooking the bay is the pleasing conversion of the old stable block. Note the circular windows and gateway: Donibristle horses were better housed than the estate workers.

Keep to the road to pass Dalgety Bay Sailing Club, and when the road swings inland, a path (by No. 37a) leads off through the Ross Plantation to Dalgety Bay itself, bird-loved mud flats at low tide, onto which it is not advisable to venture. The walk is pleasant, with Inchcolm now nearer and the mix of mud and woodland marsh, fields and gardens gives a wide variety of wildlife. (On one walk I heard woodpecker, blue tit, kestrel and eider all at once–while watching a treecreeper.) We follow round the bay (Crowhill Wood, fine gardens) to **St Bridget's Chapel**.

The miniature house at the wall is a watch house. Watch-houses were common in early Victorian days when raiding body-snatchers were selling corpses to the anatomists. The burn by the entrance was fed through basins so horses could be refreshed after their long trek to the chapel.

St Bridget's is a delight, and old, receiving its charter in 1178. Post-Reformation lairds built 'lofts' or 'ailes' (private pews in side wings) and one, upstairs, the Dunfermline Aisle, is a suite reached by a winding stair. There are some rare seventeenth-century stones and others of interest. The first on the right, entering the grounds, commemorates the drowning of a Liverpool lad of 13 in a 1799 shipwreck in the Forth. The bell is now in Aberdour Church and has the un-Presbyterian inscription: 'O mother of God remember me'. Note how some of the stones declare how many 'lairs' (spaces) are taken up. My favourite item is the table stone east of the church, where the corner scrolls are grinning faces.

Continuing from the church turn off to follow the road indicated by a SROW sign for Braefoot. This keeps along high above the sea. Don't be tempted by a branch turning down right: it leads to the local sewage works. When the big woods are reached, turn off for a worthwhile diversion, signposted for Braefoot Point. The interest here is the remains of wartime defences. A small rail line comes out from a magazine and runs out to big gun emplacements. (Test firing shattered windows across the water in Leith!) An incline goes up to anti-aircraft sites and balloon anchorages. Wander on seawards and circle left to see Braefoot and Inchcolm, a view all the better (as many are on the coast) when the trees are bare in winter.

By St Bridget's Chapel

Inchcolm from the Braefoot terminal

Incholm now lies close offshore, across Mortimer's Deep, which allows supertankers of up to 300,000 tons to nestle into the Braefoot terminal below us. The oil is pumped up to Mossmorran's huge Star Wars petro-chemical site 6km. inland. Ethylene gas is pumped onto tankers for export. Standing on top of the abbey tower on Inchcolm once, I watched a supertanker berth and its bridge was more or less on the same level.

Wander back along the spine of the headland, the works just below, then cut back to the entrance. Continue round the bend in the road till at the start of the oil site, then turn left up a straight, fenced path, between fields, to reach a small road. Turn right at the road which is lined with daffodils in season, as is all the route ahead to Aberdour. A pedestrian underpass takes us below the Braefoot terminal road.

A crossroads, en route, has a fine avenue of trees, left, and St Colm's House, right, then Downan's Plantation is a mass of snowdrops in February. Shoreward is a golf course with the Bell Rock jutting into the Forth with Aberdour Bay and the Hawkcraig beyond.

The big mast away ahead stands on the Binn. The nearer obelisk stands on Cuttle Hill and was built by the Mortons in 1744 as a landmark they could pick out from their estate at Dalmahoy in Midlothian. Our avenue reaches **Aberdour** at a set of very fine sun gates. The Woodside Hotel opposite has a bearded face on a lintel which is claimed to be of Admiral Sam Greig. As it was previously Grey's Hotel it is probably just of the original hotelier. A dominie was also a Greig. The Norwegian composer originally spelt his name the Scots way and was of Scottish descent.

If into doocots turn left, and after 250m., on the left you'll see an unusual round 'lectern' doocot. On the way back, behind a wall, is a standard 'lectern' doocot. (It's by a house with a forestair and 1713 lintel.) Both are on private property, so just look! Head on east again; there isn't much of Aberdour really, originally two villages pushed to the edges of Moray and Morton estates and split by the Dour Burn. Walk on to the 1910 Spence Memorial clock (he was a long-serving G.P.) and take the drive up to the castle but, first, look round to the right to see the seventeenth-century Aberdour House, once the Morton home, now restored as the centrepiece of a more sensitive housing estate. Before that the Mortons lived in their castle of Aberdour.

Robert the Bruce granted **Aberdour Castle** to his nephew Thomas Randolph after Bannockburn, but he sold it to a Douglas in whose ownership it remained as they clawed up to being earls. This was no sinecure: the Regent Morton–for the infant James VI–had his head cut off by the guillotine nicknamed the Maiden, which is in the Museum in Edinburgh to this day. Another Earl of Morton imprisoned Mary Queen of Scots in Loch Leven Castle. His eldest son never succeeded, as he was captured by Barbary pirates and the Civil War nearly ruined them. The original tower is ruinous now but the eastern ranges survive. However it is the setting and details that interest. There are three sundials, one from Aberdour house ('A Roman altar standing on four cannon balls'), one in the walled garden, and one up on the wall, cut into a corner to maximise the possible sunlight hours.

The gem though is a well-preserved 'beehive' doocot, one you can actually see inside. There are about 600 nesting boxes, and a revolving structure of ladders (a 'patence') allowed access to the boxes (the base can be seen in the centre of the floor), for pigeon was an important part of the diet for the well-off who alone were allowed a doocot. The pigeons ate the poor folks' grain, of course! The string courses circling the outside gave

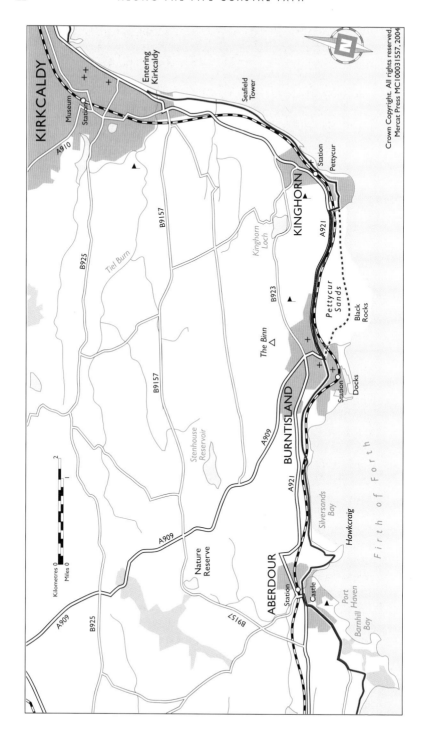

Beehive doocot at Aberdour Castle

the birds a perch, but the overhang stopped rats from entering. This doocot is sixteenth-century. Several others will be seen on our walk, Fife having been rich in 'bunnet lairds'. Beehive doocots were superseded by lectern-shaped doocots, which are quite common, usually rectangular with a single pitched roof and crowstep gables for the birds to perch on and, always, anti-rat courses. When fancier doocots were built that was the one feature kept, and always indicates a doocot.

The castle is in the care of Historic Scotland, and there's a tearoom which may be welcome. From the garden/ bowling green a gate in the east wall leads out to Hawkcraig Road, just at the drive in to the church, our next place to visit. If the gate is locked, then go round by the main road, or take a short cut through the attractive station which once won the coveted 'Best Kept' award.

As you come out onto the main road from the station the house on the slope opposite is Hillside, where another claimant to 'the second-last duel' was fought, between James Stuart of Hillside and Alexander Boswell, a son of Johnson's biographer, who was killed.

At the Drift Inn take Hawkcraig Road, signposted 'Silver Sands ¼' and just over the railway bridge is the entrance to **St Fillan's Church**, the drive of which has some interesting stones on display. First note of the church was in 1178, and a healing-well (site now unknown) made it a popular place of pilgrimage. A leper window (a narrow slit so lepers, kept safely outside, could still hear the service) is blocked by a stone addressed to pilgrims. There are some interesting stones. An inverted anchor points to being anchored in heaven. Several have rhymes, like: 'My glass is run / And yours is running / Be feared to sin / For death is coming.' Rev. Robert Blair, a famous Covenanter, is buried here. Does the architecture look a bit strange? Surely the roof is far too big? It almost reaches

Aberdour gravestone: 'Anchored in Heaven'

the ground. The clue is how one descends to the interior. The walls are normal, it's the ground that has risen, being covered with that extra depth of soil so it could continue in use as a graveyard!

Carry on down Hawkcraig Road. Local pronunciation is probably more accurate with Hawcraig (*hall craig*). There's a line of cottages, then the road swings left at a tiny dual carriageway; 100 metres on, turn right into the big car park and follow the right edge to peel off down by a very steep brae to secluded Hawkcraig House and the Viewforth Hotel: B & B's with sweeping views. The ruined pier (New Pier) used to service Inchcolm, offshore, and there's a view of bridges and Aberdour tucked in its secretive corner. At the foot of the brae, stone steps lead up onto the green dome of Hawkcraig Point, the cliffs of which are a popular rock climbing ground where the tyro can, sometimes all too literally, make a splash. Hawkcraig probably offers the most extensive view we have of the upper part of the Forth estuary. The Dour Burn flows out into the Aberdour harbour at the

Climbers on the Hawkcraig cliff

Stone Pier and old pictures show queues of holiday makers waiting to board paddle steamers. The New Pier allowed sailings at low tides.

From Hawkcraig continue down by the sea marks and onto a tarred road which leads to the **Silver Sands** car parks and other facilities. The name was dreamed up last century by the tourist publicity boys, who almost certainly didn't mention two sewage pipes running out into the bay. E.C. directives have led to the beaches being cleaned up recently, not that Fife was bad, and recently the rare sparling, or cucumber-smelt, has re-established itself in the estuary. (A shoal could be noted from the shore by the strong smell of cucumber!) The Silver Sands (a Blue Flag Beach) remains a popular corner in summer.

Aberdour crops up in an old ballad, *Sir Patrick Spens*, which gallops off with 'The king sits in Dunfermline toun, / Drinking the blude-red wine; / "O whar will I get a skeely skipper / To sail this guid ship o' mine?" ' The grim result is 'Half ower, half ower, tae Aberdour, / It's fify fathoms deep? / And thair lies guid Sir Patrick Spens / Wi the Scots Lords at his feet.' This is often taken for the journey to fetch the Maid of Norway to succeed her grandfather Alexander III (of whom more shortly), but she was taken to Orkney where she died, and the king would not have been sending for her as he was obviously alive if looking for the 'skeely skipper'. Alexander III was buried at Dunfermline. Burntisland is twinned with Flekkefjord in Norway, a modern link. (Buckhaven and Methil twin with Swedish Trelleborg and Kirkcaldy and Levenmouth with German towns.)

The path is often on the embankment of the railway (just over the wall) which runs close to the sea through this richly wooded area. A huge beech dominates the path as it goes under railway bridge 54. (They are numbered from Edinburgh.) Some dampness and water leaking onto the path indicates we've hit a limestone area. There's a spout of a spring ('well' in Scots) and then the bigger Starley Burn by the castellated bridge, which is so high in lime content it is called the Fossil Falls, as objects left in its flow soon coat over with lime. In the middle of last century there were ferocious battles, legal and physical, when the Earl of Morton tried to close the route to the public. A new body (now the Scottish Rights of Way and Access Society) was involved, and only renewed pertinacity by the public prevented the railway succeeding where landowners had failed. It even needed litigation to ensure access to the Hawkcraig and the Silver Sands.

The path runs by the curve of a wall, then joins a corkscrew road which twists down to private Carron Harbour. The path on is along the landward side of the railway. Starley Harbour, to the west, is ruined, but both these were once busy with exporting the limestone to Falkirk iron works. There are signs as we walk on of another line that brought stone from Ninelums Quarry.

The next landmark is modern enough: a huge radio mast in the field to the left of our walled way. Across the Forth we are now looking to Edinburgh, a fine silhouette from Castle to Arthur's Seat with the painted backdrop of the Pentlands beyond. (Few capitals have a hill at their hearth and a range at the doorstep.) We twist down to what was, until 2003, the most industrialised kilometre of our whole walk, a vast aluminium processing plant– which had nothing to do with the town's name, Burntisland being neither burnt nor an island. It could be a corruption of Brunty's Land or such, a *land* being a high building, as on the Royal Mile across the Forth, and Brunty/Brunton someone's name. Originally it was just Wester Kinghorn.

Alumina was extracted from bauxite imported from Ghana and brought into the harbour by barges. The red colouring once tinted the town. Red paths are made from the waste, and the flat green towards the sea here is all reclaimed land which was landscaped in 1982. Burntisland's alumina and dried hydrates went into a hundred different products, from spark-plugs to tooth-paste and pottery, to fire retardants and paints. Oil-rig construction work is now the harbour's main activity. The aluminium works closed in 2002 and the site was cleared in 2003/4 to make way for a huge new housing develop-ment. As this will take time to be finalised and will affect the FCP, a description is not possible. One will still have

Looking towards Burntisland

to pass under the railway (near a pond) to reach the reclaimed area with **Burntisland** up on the slopes ahead.
Off right is what was once a tidal mill which worked on
high tide filling a reservoir whose water was then used
on the ebb to drive the mill. At the multiple crossroads at
the foot of the hill you'll see Haddow Grove opposite.
Take the steps up behind the Haddow Grove sign, beside the houses, then turn left up what is Melville
Gardens. At the top, right, are houses in what were once
the stables of Rossend Castle (not quite as posh as
Donibristle's), dated 1816.

Rossend Castle itself stands off right as our road
swings left again (still Melville Gardens) and is an example of what can be done in the way of rescuing a ruin, in
this case one with a Mary Queen of Scots story. If every
castle seems to claim a Marian visit this is probably true
enough: both she and Queen Elizabeth in England regularly quartered the land, staying with their nobles in turn.
They had to for economic reasons, and it brought the hosts
down a bit and kept an eye on them. In 1563 an over-
romantic French courtier, Pierre de Chastelard, was
discovered hiding under the queen's bed at Rossend. As
he'd already done this at Holyrood Palace it was too
much: he was taken to St Andrews where he lost his head
in more literal fashion.

The castle was allowed to decay, especially after a
painted ceiling was taken off to the national museum,
and the local authority nearly knocked it down. Fortunately it was taken on by a firm of restoration architects
with the result we see. What would M.Q. of S. make of
drawing boards and fax machines in her bedroom? From
beside the castle, by the gazebo (folly) there's a good view
down to the harbour, one first noted by Agricola for
whom it was *portus gratiae*. Cromwell occupied
Burntisland in 1657 and built harbour defences. Pepys
noted Burntisland being bombarded by the Dutch a decade later. Mary's grandson, Charles I, has less fond
memories, crossing here in the *Dreadnought* at the end of
his coronation journey, he watched his baggage train and
many of his entourage come to grief when the *Blessing of
Burntisland* ferry capsized in a sudden squall. The treasure known to have been on board has led to current
attempts at locating the wreck. James VI on his only visit

north after the union saw a boatload of courtiers drowned in a stormy crossing.

In thick fog (October 1879) a trawler *Integrity* sank after colliding with the ferry *John Stirling*–which picked up the crew. The most scandalous sea disaster locally was the sinking of the record-breaking Cunard liner *Campania*, which had been converted into an aircraft carrier in W.W.I. Anchored a mile off Burntisland, on 5 November 1918, she snapped her anchor and drifted off to collide with three battleships in turn, *Royal Oak*, *Glorious* and *Revenge*, before the damage sank her. At 18,000 tons she is still the biggest Forth casualty.

The harbour was famous for having the world's first train ferry (1847) designed by Thomas Bouch of Tay Bridge notoriety. The actual wagons were carried across to Granton, the service eventually giving way to the Forth Bridge in 1890. Shipbuilding turned to building light aircraft carriers during the last war, but that industry failed in 1968.

Walking on we come on an archway spanning the road. The east side is more interesting with coats of arms dated 1119, 1382 and 1563. The road goes over the coast railway then, shortly after, at an opening, descend beside a car park to reach the west end of the High Street. Rail and port enthusiasts cross to go along Harbour Place and visit the harbour, such as it is (the view back has Rossend Castle perched above) and the stylish station building, a listed building. The Smugglers Inn is old and stands in a row of good restorations. Heading along the High Street, with or without this diversion, note the twin gables (of a pub) across the street, which is the town's oldest building (1671). Walk past the police station for about 30 metres then turn right through a passage with a very fine pair of marriage lintels (rescued during the tasteless 1960s reconstructions) which are dated 1626. Continue up some steps.

Somerville Square comes as quite a surprise. One of the houses has a plaque about **Mary Somerville**, briefly mentioned before as the wife of Samuel Greig, the Russian Grand Admiral. Her father was Sir William Fairfax who fought at Camperdown. Against all the odds of her time and genteel breeding, Mary became a notable scientist (largely self-educated) and had papers published on topics like 'Molecular and Microscopic Science' and 'Mechanics of the Heavens'. As a girl she was fascinated by fossils in the limestone being exported, she taught herself algebra, which led to trouble as the servants complained at her vast use of candles (were they being blamed?). Her parents discouraged her precocity, but she gradually found books and mentors before marrying her cousin and moving to London. He died shortly after and she then married another cousin, an army doctor, who gave her full support. She lived into her nineties. The Oxford college is named after her. Return from this attractive remnant by the same *pend*.

Back on the High Street you may spot a cross marked in the road–the site of the mercat cross, long gone. The library (a 1907 Carnegie gift) has a museum upstairs which is worth a visit and has in part been designed as an Edwardian showground or fair, which continues still in the summer on the Links.

From the library turn right into Kirkgate and head up it. At the first crossroads note the two carved heads up on the corner on a house dated 1886. These are taken to be Mary and Darnley or James VI and his wife or you can add your own speculation. The Church Hall occupies the end of the Kirkgate with **Burntisland Church** next to it, left, with gates which in 1992 commemorated 400 years of the church, the oldest post-reformation church in Scotland. Vandalism means gates and church are locked, but if you have made contact with the curator you'll enjoy your visit to the most interesting church of the coast.

Building a church was a precondition of James V's charter for the burgh. The church was built all square with pulpit in the centre to emphasise 'the equality of believers' but merchants and members of the crafts' guilds (hammermen, bakers, masons, wrights, etc.,) soon took gallery seats and adorned them with their arms, and the laird, of course, had to have a super-ornate pew (later the magistrates' pew). Unwilling to risk plague at St Andrews the General Assembly convened at Burntisland with James VI in attendance, and it was here in 1601 that the translation of the Bible into English was decided: the 400-year-old Authorised or King James version. The balcony can also be reached by an outside stair (a Fife feature),

Painting in the Sailors' Gallery, Burntisland Church

being a fishermen's loft, so they could enter and leave
without disturbance–presumably the tides, being God's
responsibility, allowed for this exemption. Both loft door
and main door (1592) have upside-down anchors. The
tower was a 1749 addition and the weathervane is a
gilded cockerel. The church only reopened in November
1999 after a three year restoration of the famous painted
ceiling. The nautical connection is strong, with vivid sailing galleys, battles and navigational instruments shown
on the sailors' gallery, and a model of the *Great Michael.*

In the cemetery, right round the back, is the imposing
Watson family monument with a horizontal skeleton re-
clining at the foot. The back-to-front figure 4 (Ꜣ) is a
merchants' symbol, indicating the four corners of the
world. There is a monument to an unfortunate cadger
(i.e. carrier, the figure with the barrow) who was not quite
all there, yet spent his free time, weekdays, visiting the
old and sick and giving them the minister's Sunday

sermon word for word. He was killed by a student prank which went wrong when they spiked his ale with snuff. Another stone commemorates a slave and is inscribed 'In loving remembrance of Pete (Petronella Hendrick). Born at Providence, Nickerie, Surinam… For over 60 years the faithful and devoted nurse and friend of the family of Robert Kirke…' The 'big black mama' declined to leave the family (refusing a free passage, etc.), and was remembered locally as 'a cheery buddie wi a guid Fife accent'.

Turn right leaving the church and continue along a narrowing of East Leven Street to pause before a rather ecclesiastical-looking building on the right, the 1854 Parsonage, now flats for the elderly, the work of Rev. George Hay Forbes, an 'Episcopal liturgist and publisher'. Hidden in that dry biography is another extraordinary character. He came to Burntisland, newly ordained, in 1848 and started a school (now the Inchview Hotel building). This soon grew to 90 pupils, so he built this edifice, sometimes dressing ashlars himself, though crippled with what could have been polio. (To assist movement inside he had a rope suspended which he abseiled down, and a speaking tube helped convey messages up the way). Much of his early life was bed-bound, but he learned to speak 20 languages and could read 30 more. A vast Bible translation scheme was undertaken. Ecclesiastes was his portion, translated *and* printed in 41 languages, including Hebrew, Arabic, Ethiopic, Syriac, Peshitto, Persian and Greek. On his arrival the dour people wouldn't help him up when his crutches slipped; 21 years on he was elected provost. For relaxation he'd sit at the rear of a cart, feet dangling, and have it backed into the sea so he could 'paddle'.

East Leven Street comes out at the Links, as the old common is called. In the corner, after we turn left, you'll see a cast-iron 1887 fountain with a cherub under the canopy with the town crest. See if you can find the open-jawed crocodiles on it! Across the end of the High Street is the Old Port, which stands where the East Port (gate) once gave entrance to the walled town, a very ornate, two-tone sandstone building. Salamanders flank the door; above, figures hold a shield and, higher again, there is a triple sundial with mottos: 'Time Flies', 'I mark Time, dost thou?', 'I only count the sunny hours'. Looking along you'll see the war memorial which stands at the foot of Cromwell Road. There are several options but that will do for today. Most Burntisland hotels or B & Bs lie along Kinghorn Road, eastwards, back along the High Street, or on Cromwell Road.

III
Burntisland, Kinghorn, Kirkcaldy

O.S. 66, 59

The **Burntisland Links** is our starting point, but how we go will depend on the tide. There is also the option of climbing the Binn, the 193m. hill that backs the town and gives a view quite disproportionate to its modest height. The Links themselves are occupied by the shows (travelling fair) in high summer, and the third week in July sees the local Highland Games (when local accommodation may be difficult to find). This activity dates back to the 1651 practice of horse racing (Burntisland-Kinghorn) to keep Cromwell's troops active. The silver cup was competed for till 1812. Cromwell built a fort on the Lammerlaws, the point beyond the obvious modern swimming pool complex (Beacon Centre), which replaced a one-time popular open-air pool. The windy headland was where local criminals were hung. Plague victims in 1608 were 'lodged' on the Links and Hessian troops were billeted in 1746 to counter the Young Pretender's rebellion. Wander across the Links and under the coast-hugging railway line. (Bridge 67). The sands here once were crowded with holidaymakers. An Edwardian photograph shows police having to do crowd control for a sandcastle competition! Turn left to walk to the end of the promenade. The building there was once a popular tearoom.

If miles of sand stretch away out to some rocks (the Black Rocks) then make the most of this and rim round the margin of the sea to Pettycur and Kinghorn. Stumps of posts in the sand were wartime defences against any *airborne* landing. Each June there is a popular Black Rock Race from Kinghorn round the skerry and back. The starting time depends on the state of the tide!

If the sea is lapping up to make shore access impossible, go under the railway again (Bridge 69) and turn right along the main road past the Kingswood Hotel, the Alexander III monument and the sprawl of Pettycur Bay caravan park, left. At the Sandhills caravan park, right,

Walking out to the Black Rocks off Burntisland

take the enclosed footpath down to Pettycur Bay and harbour. If the tide is out or falling the vast Pettycur sands would be the most rewarding choice: miles of pristine sands with Inchkeith anchored out in the estuary and Edinburgh off to starboard.

The Kingswood Hotel is renowned and there is a big restaurant, café, swimming pool and shop complex at the Pettycur Bay Holiday Park, while Kinghorn has cafés on its High Street. The obelisk to Alexander III, last of the Celtic kings, should not be missed. He rode over the cliffs (grey conglomerates) here one wild night in 1286, bringing to an end a sort of Golden Age and creating one of the great *ifs* of history. If only he had had patience and sired a male heir. If only he hadn't insisted in crossing the Queen's ferry that afternoon, against all advice, if only he hadn't set off in stormy dusk for his castle, and new queen Yolande, at Kinghorn. He was found dead at the foot of the cliffs next morning. His granddaughter and heir, Margaret, the Maid of Norway, died in Orkney on the way back to Scotland, thereby leaving the succession wide open to clamorous claimants. Edward I, asked to arbitrate, said he'd have it himself, which led to the Wars of Independence, Bruce and Bannockburn, the Stewarts (who ironically, became England's monarchs) and all of history since…

The alternative or addition which is particularly pleasing early or late is to go up **the Binn**. Never Binn Hill please; that is tautology, Binn being the murdered Gaelic for hill. One can do an hour's round of the Binn or traverse it and reach Kinghorn cross-country. Either way head off up Cromwell Road and straight on at the roundabout (Cowdenbeath A909 road) to leave Burntisland. The houses on the right are followed by a field and this by a wood where, almost at once, there is a way in signposted 'Public footpath to Standing Stanes Road'. Follow this path up the wood and across an open field to a gate, then, just 25m. on, turn right for the 'Public footpath to the Bin' (*sic*). A small dam is passed, home to coots and ducks, while the woods have laughing *yaffles* (green woodpeckers) and there are often buzzards wheeling and mewing overhead.

A green road leads on from the gate, curving up towards the big mast, but leave this to swing right to reach the edge of the hill, soon craggy to the south, but giving a splendid ridge walk. There are stiles at field edges and the summit has a view indicator. The big mast lies further inland with the twin paps of the Lomonds behind. They and the Binn are remnants of volcano activity. The Binn rock is extremely friable, and all sorts of barriers and hanging mesh (old submarine defence nets) have been installed, though now trees are probably as good a protection for the houses below. If the tide is out you'll see the huge sweep of the Pettycur sands edged by the Black Rocks. The whole estuary lies mapped out up to the bridges and we have a bold view of the Bass Rock far

On the Binn

down the Lothian shore. Burntisland has two mottoes on its crest: *Portus Gratiae* (the Romans recognised the 'safe harbour') and *Colles praesidio dedit Deus*, 'God gave the hills for protection'.

Continue the traverse along by the wind-gnarled thorns. The red area ahead is the recycling centre for the waste from the aluminium works, and on the near edge of it, swallowed in nettles and growing trees, is the site of the Binn village. There are people alive who once lived there, a population of 1000, with a school, mission hall etc. From the Binn, across under the Forth and much of the Lothians, the ground is honeycombed with the workings of the once vital shale oil industry. The Binn boomed in 1878, but when easier, cheaper oil was struck in America it was the death knell to Scotland's shale oil works. The Binn was closed down in 1905, but it was popular with holidaymakers for two decades when the *William Muir* ferry brought them over from the capital.

Follow field edges to the overgrown area (the Binn village site) just before the big wire fence of the works area. There is a gate and the track runs on outside the boundary fence, once a mineral line, which is the Kinghorn continuation. If returning to Burntisland turn down right just before the fence and follow a footpath down to the Burntisland-Kirkcaldy road. Turn right, pass the golf club and head down into the town, back to the roundabout and Cromwell Road.

Binn village as it used to be

The continuation loses height very gently to reach and angle left across the original Burntisland—Kirkcaldy road, and some care is advised in crossing. The track on is signposted (SRWAS) and wends through fields (views to Kinghorn Loch and back to the Binn), passing right of the Black Acre farm buildings, then Grangehill House, to come out to Kinghorn Golf Course. Follow the track through this and pass the club house to exit onto the A921 road. Turn left along to the centre of **Kinghorn**.

The building on the landward side facing the imposing war memorial was the offices of Gibson's, the first golf-club manufacturer in Scotland. At its peak, 100 dozen hand-forged heads a week were turned out. Turn right at the war memorial onto Pettycur Road (which goes all the way down to Pettycur Harbour). Note the old primary school with its restored clock tower, now the town's community centre and library. Turn first left, into Harbour Road, where we join up with the route along the Burntisland—Kinghorn sands or the A921. Steps, left, lead up to the railway station: a station with a view.

The miles of sand from Burntisland end at Pettycur Bay, where the path down from the A921 joins in. Modern houses now back the bay on what was once a bottleworks site, and, before that, salt works. The crags above have a prow, Witches' Point, where these unfortunates were burned (the last in 1644), just outside a cemetery. Before the cemetery there was a leech loch which mysteriously drained away, long before the coast road was built in 1842 or the railway cut through Kinghorn. There are a lot of Polish names on the stones, as their forces were based in Fife during the war. Many stones are flat, being blown over by the great gale of February 1968, a gale which blocked every possible route out of Fife as I found out.

Pettycur has a single, rather battered 1760 harbour arm with a few boats and huts, contrasting with its history as an important ferry. Storms damaged the original harbour in 1625 and it silted up badly. (There are 17 steps in the corner, for instance–but how many can you count?) A prize of £1000 was offered to solve this problem of silting, and the answer was to build a tidal pool where the car park is now and, at low tide, to let this out in a spate which washed away the accumulated sand. Kinghorn originally was the town up along the High Street and running down to the next bay; Pettycur was the ferry area and, all across Fife, milestones are made out to Pettycur, to the puzzlement of many. Alexander III's castle stood up above the harbour somewhere, on what was Crying-oot Hill. I suspect this was from a message being yelled up to the town pubs to say the next ferry was coming in. Pettycur is one of the *pit-/pet-* prefixes indicating Pictish origins, and not *petit coeur* as I've heard suggested. Kinghorn has nothing to do with kings or horns. The first part is *ceann*, meaning head, *gorn* was a marsh (Kinghorn loch?). A thirteenth century map has it Kyngorn.

Take the road up from Pettycur Harbour whose importance as a ferry lasted till the railway ferry years. The road curves up and, if followed, leads to the High Street. The once-popular novelist Annie S. Swan lived on Pettycur Road. Turn off at a footway with the odd name of Doodells Lane (a corruption of 'two delfs', an old local measure) which leads one round above Kinghorn Bay where the parish church can be seen. At one time there was a shipyard beyond, specialising in ferry boats. Quarrel Brae refers to the battle when Macbeth and Banquo defeated a Danish invasion force. During Henry VIII's 'Rough Wooing' and the Battle of Pinkie (1547) the English burnt Kinghorn and killed over 400 people. Cromwell did much the same.

Kinghorn

The path comes out at Harbour Road. Turn down this, but if wanting the town, or the view, the steps opposite go up to Kinghorn station with the town inland of the line. We walk down and then the route turns up under the arches but, before that, turn down to visit the church which, though hardly impressive, is quite historic (1774 on a thirteenth-century base) and gives a viewpoint over Kinghorn Bay. If you peer through the nearest window you can see a 1569 ship model hanging in the Sailors' Aisle. One gravestone has the symbol of a plough on it and another relates to a Kirkcaldy tragedy described later: 'Alexander [Dougal], aged 13, who suffered among many others by the fall of a gallary (sic) in Kirkcaldy's church, 15th June 1828'. (The Dougal family had already lost two boys, aged one and eight.) One Kinghorn minister's wife, thought to be dead, was buried alive and only recovered when the sexton was struggling to steal the rings from her cold fingers. Another stone marks the grave of a victim of the Tay Bridge disaster. Kinghorn's most forgotten person of note is Christina Robertson (1796—1854), who became a famous portrait painter. She was court painter to Tsar Nicholas I, but died as the Crimea War began and in the following years was simply forgotten.

Heading back up under the arches of the striding 1846 viaduct (Nethergate) there is a childrens' play area where the signposted path leads off right to head for Kirkcaldy. The path goes under the railway then runs awhile between railway and a caravan park to reach a bay with some curious names. The inlet at the far end is Hoch-ma-toch and the town end is called Bellypuff. The old shipyard was near there. As there was no dock, ships had to be launched completed and with steam up. Engines came by train and the overhead crane transferring them was made from girders retrieved from the Tay Bridge disaster. The yard closed in 1922. They'd built ferries for the Granton-Burntisland run.

The rocks at the far end of the bay are lavas which have flowed from the Binn; you can almost see their movement and expect the sea to hiss with steam. Underneath are the obvious levels of limestone and shale, all displayed for the geology lesson. A well, easily overlooked, descending, once refreshed working horses and drouthy cadgers.

The path zigzags up to gain height, running close by

the railway to reach steps up to a wall at the highest point, an extensive viewpoint over the Forth. The Fife Coastal Path runs on through thorn thickets beside the railway and then angles down towards the ruin of Seafield Tower. Below this slope lies the secretive Seafield Cave, a narrow slot running in over 100 feet, redolent of smuggling days and probably the deepest cave on the coast. It was originally longer, but railway construction in 1847 caused a collapse. Low tide gives access. To visit the cave without backtracking from near the castle, turn down the east side of the wall to a rougher path which descends to the bridge that spans the entrance, a bridge renewed in 2003 through the efforts of the Kirkcaldy Civic Society. Beyond are thickets of thorn and the faint remains of limekilns which lead on towards the castle. The rocks offshore often have seals on them and the coast can be lively with migrant wading birds. Just above the tideline before the castle there is a spring which may have served the castle, the seat of the Moultrays. The last of the family perished in the 1715 Rising and the castle was abandoned thereafter.

From the castle a gritty road leads on, passing a big harbour arm, built in 1889 but never used thanks to disputes–and who would want a harbour set among all those reefs (a steamship, *Adam Smith*, ran aground on them on Boxing Day 1884), reefs much loved by seals who will be heard 'singing' in season. A ruined brick culvert takes the Tyrie Burn to the sea. The Tyrie bleach-

Heading towards Seafield Tower

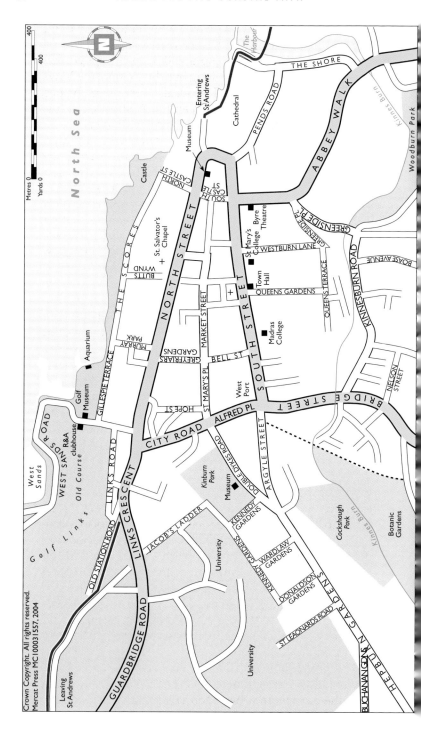

works once employed 70 people who regularly walked there from Kinghorn or Kirkcaldy along what is our coastal path. There was also a 400m. long ropeworks' building further on, a long, long building where the hawsers were twisted together. This scruffy, rocky stretch once had popular sands with Punch and Judy shows, but human alterations led to the sea washing it all away.

The most recent industry to come and go was mining. Where the houses stand up on the left there were once the twin winding towers of the Seafield Colliery (seen in the picture on p.51) which only opened in 1954–and some of us watched the towers toppled by an explosion in 1988. Much of the area has been landscaped, with a parking area and an extensive grassy area above the better sands. Entering, there are the Coastal Path notices, etc. Ahead, the stands and floodlights of Starks Park, Raith Rovers' football stadium, can be seen.

Continuing, the *official* path exits by the access road to join the main coast road, right, and right at the roundabouts to swing onto the **Kirkcaldy** esplanade, but an *unofficial* line keeps along by the grassy verge of the shore to reach the Tiel Burn, then turns up its bank to nip over a wall onto the esplanade. If the tide is well out one can simply walk away along the shore and aim for the steps where the esplanade wall bulges out. You'll see why Kirkcaldy is called the Lang Toon. But did you know, 'The deil's deid and burried in Kirkcaldy'? One of the many stories concerning Michael Scott ('The Wizard') is a battle he had with the devil who plagued him, nightly, for work, which he always grimly performed and came back for more. Scott finally was rid of him: he told him to come down to the shore here and make an endless rope of sand.

At the start (south end) of the esplanade, overlooking the Tiel Burn, is a big car park with a snack bar and toilets. 'South end' may cause raised eyebrows, and local people too all talk of the east or west end of the High Street or esplanade when the town lies north south due to the curvature of the big bay. It is almost as surprising to discover Kirkcaldy is further west than Carlisle, or Liverpool.

The promenade should be followed to the first set of traffic lights. Cross there onto Nicol Street. On the right side the garden area has been created in what was the

Volunteers Green, a training area for the Napoleonic 'Territorial Army'. Cannons faced out to sea. They might have come in following the raid by John Paul Jones. He anchored offshore and threatened to bombard the town unless paid £200,000, a lot of money in 1778. The Rev. Robert Shirra went down to the Pathhead Sands and led prayers for the town's deliverance. An offshore gale promptly blew the marauder away.

At the next set of traffic lights turn right onto the High Street and through another set to reach the pedestrianised part of the town. The traffic swings left, into Whitecauseway, where the Tourist Information Office is found. You could say you are in the centre of Kirkcaldy, which is pronounced something like Curr-coddy. Town signs proclaim it the birthplace of Adam Smith.

A High Street plaque indicates his mother's house where he wrote the seminal *Wealth of Nations*. He was born in Kirkcaldy in 1723. At the age of three he was kidnapped from Strathendry Castle by tinkers. One of the stalwarts of the Scottish enlightenment, he was a friend of people like David Hume and Robert Adam, the latter another Kirkcaldy lad. William Adam (b.1689) was the son of a Kirkcaldy mason who became a big-time entrepreneur in coal, salt, milling, brewing, land and farming besides creating the masterpieces of Haddo, Mellerstain, Hopetoun, House of Dun and Tingwall. Even so he was to be overshadowed by his son Robert, and Robert's three brothers. Robert was born in 1728, but his schooling was disrupted by 'the Forty-five' and he travelled on the continent for some years. By the time he died in 1792, his buildings, monuments and fortifications ranged from Kent to Antrim and Cornwall to Fort George, and his influence remains to this day.

The town's oddest famous literary figure of that period was a girl who died at the age of eight. Marjory Fleming's *Diary* has seldom been out of print since. (New complete *Mercat Press* edition in 1999.) She might have been forgotten had not Dr John Brown (of *Rab and His Friends* etc) romanticised her story, made her a friend of Sir Walter Scott and called her 'Pet' Marjorie as she is described on her portrait memorial in Abbotshall churchyard. My favourite symbol stone in that cemetery is one of crossed rake and spade, indicating a gardener.

Kirkcaldy's most ancient historical figure is Michael Scott, a whizz kid of the thirteenth century, a scholar at Oxford, Paris and Toledo and Professor of Rhetoric at Bologna, philosopher, doctor, Arabic scholar, mathematician and chemist. He was nicknamed The Wizard and incredible stories accrued about him–such as that he cleft the Eildons into three (the Romans called them Trimontium a millennium earlier).

Kirkcaldy's most modern sporting hero is now largely forgotten.

Marjory Fleming's memorial

John Thomson played football for the local coal mine team and was signed up by a scout who'd come to watch the opponent's goalkeeper. He played in several cup-winning teams, but in 1931, playing for Celtic in an Old Firm meeting, he dived at the feet of an attacker and received a kick which proved fatal.

Wheels within wheels: Marshall Keith (a Jacobite exile whose family name gives the island off Kirkcaldy its name of Inchkeith) was once involved in peace negotiations with the Turks, in Turkey, on behalf of Russia (with the commissioners and translators all conducting business with great solemnity). Business over, the Turkish vizier then took the Marshall aside and welcomed him in thick Kirkcaldy accents. The vizier's father had been town bellman and he had 'spied they Keiths in the toon whan they wis aw chiels the gither'.

A plaque in the Town House mentions six famous sons of Kirkcaldy: Robert Adam, Adam Smith, Robert Philp, Dr John Philip, Sandford Fleming and John MacDouall Stuart. Stuart will be mentioned later, Sir Stanford Fleming was an engineer who surveyed the Canadian

Kirkcaldy Town House

Pacific Railway and the inventor of world Standard Time, Philp and Philip were related but not happily. Philp was a rich linen-manufacturer and philanthropist who was very annoyed when relatives changed the spelling of the name. 'If ma name isna guid enough for thems, then neither is ma siller.' Doctor John was the first superintendent of the London Missionary Society, and it was to him Doctor David Livingstone reported on his arrival in South Africa.

Walking up Whitecauseway from the Tourist Office/ High Street, one comes to the Town Hall. Turn right at the crossroads and walk along behind it to see the collection of six decorative old Provost's lamps from the burghs that 'died' in the 1975 changes to local administration: Burntisland, Kirkcaldy, Dysart, Buckhaven and Methil, Leven, Markinch and Leslie. (Leslie had no lamp.) The bus-station is opposite. The town hall was started in 1939 and completed after the war. Wall sculpture and green copper spire are notable and there's a large stair mural. Head on, inland, from there and cross at the roundabout ahead.

Right lies the Adam Smith Centre (a Carnegie gift), a complex of theatre, halls and café, left is the war memorial garden, always a showpiece (as is the large Beveridge Park, at the west side of the town) overlooked by the Library and award-winning Museum and Art Gallery. Walk through the gardens. The war memorial itself has a horrifying number of names on it (over 1350). John Nairn, of the linoleum family, gifted the integrated site to be the town's memorial. After the big commercial attractions like Sea World, the Museum and Art Gallery is Fife's largest tourist attraction, which speaks for itself. The museum is well planned (note the furniture made of *coal*!), and there are several exhibitions a year in the galleries, besides the more permanent displays, particularly rich in works by William McTaggart, S J Peploe and E A Hornel. The café is popular too. The most popular exhibition in the last few years was on Peploe and the contemporary Jack Vettriano from Leven. Posters of his strange work outsell Monet or Van Gogh and have made the former miner a millionaire. The stone for the building came from the Grange Quarry on the Binn at Burntisland.

The railway station lies behind the museum, a modern building following a fire caused by vandals. What changes? Burntisland station was burned down by vandals in 1914. On the wall by the station is a Victorian (VR) letterbox. A public outcry saw it put back when an attempt was made to install a replacement. In the station a popular old poem hangs on the wall about taking the train to Kirkcaldy. The last couplet goes, 'For I ken mysel' by the queer-like smell / That the next stop's Kirkcaldy!' Linoleum is still manufactured in a small way, so occasionally there is the nice smell of hot linseed oil on the air. A few more comments on people and places as we set off from the town is held for the next section.

48

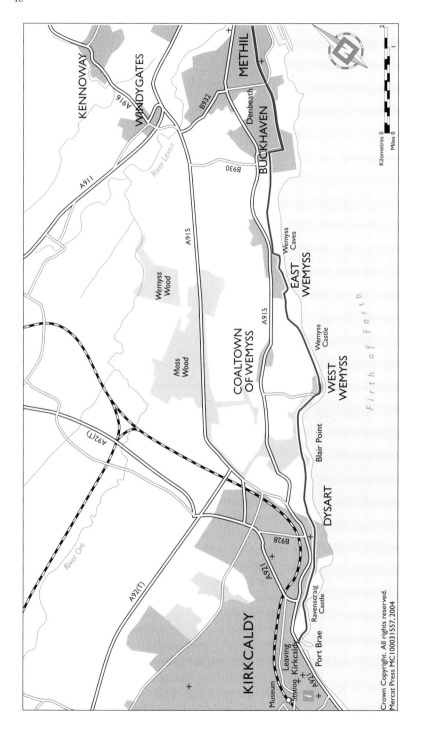

KENNOWAY

WINDYGATES

METHIL

A916

B932

Denbeath

BUCKHAVEN

River Leven

B930

A911

A915

Wemyss Caves

EAST WEMYSS

Wemyss Wood

A915

COALTOWN OF WEMYSS

Wemyss Castle

Moss Wood

WEST WEMYSS

Firth of Forth

A92(M)

Blair Point

River Ore

DYSART

B928

A921

A92(T)

Ravenscraig Castle

KIRKCALDY

Port Brae

Leaving Kirkcaldy

A921

Stop

Museum

Kilometres 0   2

Miles 0   1

IV
The Old Coal Coast
(Dysart to Leven)
O.S. 59

This is quite a long day's walk with some inescapable pavement pounding, but a surprising number of interesting places milestone the route, so there has had to be a selection rather than detailed coverage. Variety is the Spice of Fife.

Picking up the route at the Kirkcaldy Tourist Office end of the pedestrianised High Street, head along it. Tolbooth Street, right, has no tolbooth now. Kirk Wynd, left, ends the pedestrianised stretch and is the only bit of Kirkcaldy with any appearance of antiquity. The Old Kirk (the parish church) was consecrated in 1244 but only the tower dates back to that time. Below it a Victorian house incorporates battlements, turrets, coat-of-arms, the lot, even a dragon on the gully box. Next door is a typical old house with crow-step gables and red pantiles and MA/ML marriage lintel (Matthew Anderson, a corn merchant, and Margaret Livingstone). A plaque (same side, further on) notes 'Thomas Carlyle lodged here 1816—1818. His school is opposite'. This old burgh school has long gone. Another who taught there under Carlyle was Edward Irving, the famous preacher. Their tangled lives almost deserve Big Screen treatment. Irving graduated at 17 and took a teaching post at Haddington. He tutored Jane Welsh, the doctor's daughter, and fell in love with her when she was only thirteen while he was already engaged to the minister's daughter. He introduced Jane to Thomas Carlyle and *they* eventually married; and both have lasting fame. Irving after 12 years grudgingly married his determined fiancée. He became assistant to Thomas Chalmers, one of the ecclesiastical giants of the time, but left for London to become a popular preacher. His excesses led to his being excommunicated, so he formed his own church. He had one last, tragic, contact with Kirkcaldy. In 1807 a huge horseshoe gallery had been made out of the old guilds' lofts in the parish church, and when he preached there in 1828 the crowd was so great the north gallery collapsed and 28 people died in the accident or resulting panic. Irving and Carlyle once *rowed* from Kirkcaldy to visit Inchkeith.

The church had the spire blown off the tower on Christmas Eve 1900, and in 1968 the galleries were removed and the inside remodelled, only for a vandal's fire in 1986 requiring much new restoration work. (A taxi driver saw smoke coming from the tower in the early hours of the morning and raised the alarm.) The chancel windows are by Burne-Jones, and the contemporary west windows are striking, slender columns of colour and light.

Kirkcaldy only became the major local town with the Industrial Revolution, but a church stood here back in the earliest days. Large populations often meant lively religious life, with churches dominating every aspect of social behaviour. Kirkcaldy threw up many famous ministers, and to this day there are over 40 varied places of worship; beside the large denominations you can find everything from the Apostolic Church to Zionists, via Mormons, Jehovah's Witnesses, Brethren, Quakers, Spiritualists, the Salvation Army and Scotland's only Coptic church. There's also a mosque.

The High Street goes on to meet the Esplanade, or strictly speaking the Esplanade joins the High Street, for the coastal A955 is still High Street along to the harbour, now hardly in use. Facing the harbour is Sailors' Walk, the oldest surviving house in the town, dating to c.1460. Both Charles II (after his Scone Coronation) and Mary Queen of Scots stayed here. The harbour was built for whaling rather than general trade or fishing, and was at its busiest when importing cork for the linoleum manufacturing which dominated inland from the harbour area for a century. In 1644 Kirkcaldy had 100 ships registered, then came the Civil War: 200 local men died at the Battle of Kilsyth in 1645, and five years later 480 died defending the town against Cromwell's troops when 50 ships were lost. A few years later only 12 ships were registered. We forget the past horrors. In 1584 plague killed 300 Kirkcaldy people. Hutchison flour mills now dominate as we puff up the steep Path into **Pathhead**. The brae is pronounced *peth* and its original snaking steepness was a challenge and danger to horse-drawn traffic. (The minister, Mr

Stormy seas at Kirkcaldy

Martin, Edward Irving's long-suffering father-in-law, was for instance fatally thrown from his carriage in 1827.)

There is quite a *den* (dale, glen) inland here, all unnoticed, once the haunt of a young John Buchan whose father was a minister in Pathhead and only left for Glasgow when JB was fourteen. His sister, novelist O. Douglas, was born here. The opening scene of *Prester John* is set on Pathhead Sands and steps down may have inspired the 39. *The Free Fishers* starts with the nail-makers and weavers of Pathhead. The house at the top, Path House, is seventeenth-century and attractive (there's a two-faced sundial) and modern houses have been made to agree with it, unlike the tower blocks beyond.

Near Path House is the Feuars burial-ground (locked because of vandalism) which has a connection with the Porteous Riots in Edinburgh in 1736. Andrew Wilson was a baker in Flesh Wynd and did some smuggling on the side. 'English' taxes on Scotland after the 1707 Union encouraged this. Wilson and a friend, Robertson, robbed a custom's officer at Pittenweem, were caught and condemned to be hanged in Edinburgh. Taken to church for their last service, Wilson seized their guards and yelled at Robertson to run for it. With some help from the congregation he made his escape. Next day Wilson was hanged and the irate mob stoned the guards. Captain Porteous, a weak, lazy bully of a man ordered them to open fire and several people were killed. He was tried in turn, condemned to death, then reprieved, which so enraged public opinion that a mob broke in to his quarters, dragged him off and hanged him from a dyestaff in the Grassmarket.

Continue along the main road to bear right at the roundabout (A955, Dysart Road) and take the first entrance, right, into **Ravenscraig Park**, then right again to wend along to Ravenscraig Castle. The castle on its prow of red sandstone dominates bays to both sides, and was the romantic setting for Scott's *Lay of the Last Minstrel*. From here the unfortunate Rosabelle set off over the Forth, only to be drowned. Sadly the castle is no longer maintained as its historical position deserves. There is no custodian and some of the best features are locked because, unsurprisingly, vandalism is rife.

Ravenscraig Castle was the first to be built to cope with the new weapon of attack, cannon. In places the walls are 14 feet thick and the slanting roof was designed to deflect cannon balls. Ironically, the castle's creator, James II, was killed by a cannon exploding when he was laying siege to Roxburgh Castle. Ravenscraig was completed by his widow, Mary of Gueldres, but soon passed to the Sinclair family, who owned it till 1896. The prow has a small cave at the seaward end, which was once bigger but much of the roof fell in, in 1740, killing ten boys. The warnings at the Wemyss Caves should be heeded.

Ravenscraig Castle

Walk back to Ravenscraig Park and turn right to follow
its seaward edge through to Dysart. The first path, off
right, descends to the beehive doocot, worth the diversion to see this well-preserved sixteenth-century rarity.
Return to the park rim and on to pass the pepperpot
corner turret on the boundary wall. This wall weaves in
and out in a rather ridiculous manner, following every
indentation of the coast, and was built by the spiteful
laird to stop miners walking along the shore to work. The
Earl of Rosslyn was so unpopular that the masons came
back at night to knock down their own labours. The park
was his demesne and linked to Dysart House, his home,
by a private bridge. Irony there too, for Rosslyn had to
sell everything to pay off enormous gambling debts, and
the new owners, the Nairns, gifted the park to the town.
The small tower jutting out on the wall is a good spot to
watch wintering waders on the rocks below.

Eventually a breach in the wall is reached, with several options for the walker: to pass outside and along the
lawn, to follow a low path, inside, where the wall goes
on, or, best, to go up the brae for a path giving the best
views. Doing this last, soon turn right at a junction and
on to a track that circles round right, suddenly to open up
the **Dysart** view, much painted by artists: St Serf's Tower,
Pan Ha' and the harbour right below. At a gap in the
wall go down the steps to the railed balcony path of the
Sailors' Walk and turn right to descend to the harbour.

The inner harbour was cut down into solid rock and
opened in 1831. Much of the waste was dumped in the
sea to the west (the tunnel gave access for carts) where
tides soon washed it into the harbour entrance. Coal came
from local mines and carts would queue up to fill the
holds; a cargo could be 250 cart-loads.

The road up from the harbour is Hot Pot Wynd, a corruption of the Dutch word for a brae (*het pat*). The
Netherlands connection was such that Dysart folk were
called Little Hollanders. A Carmelite Monastery now
occupies Dysart House (up Hot Pot Wynd). The area beyond the harbour is tidied up with grass and car parks,
but once was a major site for salt production, a dirty, la-
borious business: it took 32 tons of sea water and 16 tons
of coal to produce one ton of salt. Water was pumped
from the sea into huge pans and boiled over coal fires till

Pan Ha', Dysart

the water evaporated. Pan Ha' is from Pan Haugh, the level ground where the pans operated. The Fife coast was a major salt-producer because coal was so readily available. Salt and coal, beer and fish all went to the Low Countries and the return imports included cartwheels, Delftware, kegs of Hollands, pipes of Rhenish and the familiar pantiles. There was much trade with Scandinavia and Germany too. Scotland has always been European in a way England never was.

Coal made Dysart a prosperous town, but at a price. There were awful accidents. In 1476 the town nearly vanished in an explosion; there was another in 1578 and multiple deaths in 1662, 1700, 1791... By 1912 over 900 miners were employed in the Lady Blanche, the Frances (Sinclair names) and Randolph (a Wemyss name). A tunnel brought coal from the first right to the port and also acted as a ventilation shaft, as did an older stair pit, the Violet. A 'stair pit' was just that; after the coal was 'putted' (pulled) to the foot of the shaft it was carried up on the backs of women and children, who worked 12 hours a day. Miners were no better than serfs until 1799, when some alleviating legislation began.

The castle-like tower is of St Serf's church, little of which remains. The north aisle was removed to make the road down to the harbour. Before the Reformation the local priest Walter Myln was arrested and burnt at the stake in St Andrews for heresy. In 1642 a Margaret

Young was imprisoned in the tower for ten weeks on a charge of witchcraft. That was a nasty century. Town minutes of 1633 record monies paid out for dealing with two witches: 'For 10 loads of coal to burn them, For a tar barrell, For towes, To the executioner, To him that brought the executioner, For the executioner's expenses, £14. 4s. 6d'. In 1649 the Dysart minister, an 'expert', was called to Burntisland to test a witch by sticking a pin into her flesh, and the result was proof of guilt, so she was burned the same day.

Walk along the attractive row of red-roofed, white harled houses, restored in the 1960s under the National Trust for Scotland's 'Little Houses Scheme', which saved many small dwellings on the Fife coast. The first building was once the Bay Horse Inn. There's a dated lintel (1583) round the back, part of the old manse, inscribed, 'My hoip is in the Lord'. The reef offshore is the Partan Craig, 'partan' being the edible crab. Alleys leading up from the houses are Saut Girnal Wynd (salt store lane) and Hie Gate (high lane). Go up the latter, climbing past the 1582 house, the Anchorage, to a junction. Rectory Lane, heading up opposite has, on the right, the museum to John MacDouall Stuart, the first person to have crossed Australia south to north in 1861-62. Born in Dysart in 1815, he emigrated in 1839. He was on Captain Sturt's expedition five years later, then mounted expeditions of his own to Lake Eyre and the centre of Australia. Two previous attempts on the complete south-north had failed, so his ultimate 2000-mile journey was quite a feat. He returned by the same route.

Walk on up Rectory Lane and turn first right onto the High Street. The centre has an ornate lamp erected in 1887 for Queen Victoria's Jubilee. Beyond is the attractive old tolbooth with an outside stair and the date 1576, when it was probably first erected. The Town House stair (next door, 1617) shows a simplified version of the town's crest, a bare tree with exposed roots. In 1840 there was a report of the prison in the tolbooth being 'quite unsuitable... dry, but not very secure'. Cromwell stored gunpowder in the tower and an accident 'blowed off the roofe... so scarcely remained a sclait'. We continue straight on but, if enthusiastic for Fife's old buildings, turn left up Cross Street to Quality Street to see a superbly restored building,

The Towers, dated 1586. The house next door has a 1610 marriage lintel.

Heading on from the town centre, the High Street becomes Edington Place, with villas on the left. When the road turns sharp left at a modern housing scheme, keep straight on. A well-fenced footpath runs along past the site of the one-time Frances colliery with its remnant winding tower. Both the Frances here and the Michael (3k. ahead) were finally worked from the Seafield at Kirkcaldy. All have gone, virtually without trace. The grassy area to the right of the path disguises the waste tip, the redd being simply dumped into the sea, which is still eroding this coast. The Dubbie Braes, as this area was called before the Frances opened, was a popular spot a century ago with picnics and preachings, political meetings, cricket, dancing and hiking all popular. There was a bandstand. The Volunteers practised firing at a target offshore. Everything was tidied up for Victoria's Jubilee (public wash-house removed etc) when there was an all day (and night) party. The Frances destroyed all that– and now it too has gone.

Follow the fence line on round past the back of an industrial estate in from Blair Point. There's a brief view of open sea before steps plunge the path down to shore level again, with a sweep of bay leading to pretty West Wemyss. Under Blair Point the 'Red Rocks' (where witches were burnt) have crumbled into the sea, in 1971 taking with them a weaver's 1851 carving illustrating Byron's *Prisoner of Chillon*, known as *The Man in the Rock*. The shore path round west to Dysart has long gone.

The bay ahead is shingly, though at one time sandy. Mining subsidence caused the sand to be washed away. The bay is backed by Chapel Wood; any water running out is rusty red, probably from old mineworkings with which the area is riddled. Flints found on the shore came from ballast tipped out at West Wemyss harbour. Our path joins a rough drive with an old tower half-hidden behind a wall with grilled arches, everything creepy with trees. Hitchcock could have made use of the location, which is actually the burial ground of the Wemyss family. The first chapel may be a fifteenth-century one built by Spaniards fleeing the Inquisition. The chapel was destroyed at the Reformation, but in 1627 Lord Elcho (later second Earl of Wemyss) turned it into a house. The First World War Admiral of the Fleet and First Sea Lord, Lord Wemyss is probably the most notable person buried here. The track passes below a slope covered in teasels (and old allotments) to pass between a white house and red cliffs.

The harbour of **West Wemyss** dates back to the early sixteenth century at least. (In 1590 a barque from plague-infected England put in and passed on the dreaded epidemic.) The white building (Shorehead House, sixteenth-century) has a Dutch gable and is the one-time pilot's house, always painted white to act as a seamark. The harbour has been largely filled in and landscaped, but do walk round to the end of the harbour arm for the view. The Victoria pit was sited here, but ran out of coal in 1914. East of Shorehead House the bricked-up arches are the site of the pit pony stables. Another bricked-up arch is a tunnel which went 1km. up to the Hugo Mine at Coaltown of Wemyss, which then was linked to Methil docks by rail. The tunnel kept the mining activities decently out of sight of Wemyss Castle. It was bricked up after some school kids became lost in it and nearly died. The building above the houses as we walk on is the Belvedere Hotel, created in what was the Miners' Institute; built in 1927, closed in 1952 and converted in 1979. There are some interesting old local photographs on the walls, including those showing the damage from a great storm in 1898.

East, West and Coaltown of Wemyss were built as mining villages. Sadly, with the failure of mining, West Wemyss slipped into decay, its architectural worth ignored until recently. The Coxstool buildings looking onto the harbour offer a fine example of restoration work, however. Coal was exported largely to Middlesborough, Amsterdam and Hamburg. In 1901 West Wemyss had a population of 1,300; in 1981 it was 379. Methil Docks, opened in 1887 to serve steamships, also contributed to the decline of the smaller, older ports. Head off along Main Street, which has been attractively restored.

Dutch influence is seen in the slender tower of the tolbooth with its swan weathervane (the oft-repeated logo of the Wemyss family) and a corner cut away and with a 'pal stone' at its foot to protect the corner from damage by passing wheels. The pend (passage) leads through to what was Duke Street, a corruption of *joug*, meaning jail.

The street has been used as a location for a TV serial. I like the name Happies Close (right) near the end of Main Street. The war memorial occupies an old entrance to the churchyard and there's a turning area for vehicles beside the present entrance.

St Adrian's is built of red sandstone with a bold, round west window. Adrian was an early Christian missionary who may have come from Hungary originally. He founded a chapel on the May Island but was killed by a Viking raid c. 850. On going in one sees some pathetic marble monuments to children and, past the door, left, to 'sons John, Alex and James who fell in action in France. 1915. 1916. 1917'. Behind the church is a stone made of parrot coal and one with the crown of a hammerman. Against the back wall a big 4 indicates a merchant. And there's a stone with the date of death as 31st April 1878!

Walking on, the view is dominated by Wemyss Castle, a rather bleak-looking pile. A walled-up cave in the first crag is known as Green Jean's Cave after the ghost who appears when there is a death in the castle. (She appeared rather often when the castle was a wartime hospital.) It was at Wemyss Castle Mary Queen of Scots first met Lord Darnley–with all that followed.

Once past the castle policies we are briefly diverted onto the shore itself. There's an old harbour arm ahead with Buckhaven behind (the construction yard obvious) and Largo Law against the skyline. The path runs behind an isolated rock, called the Lady Rock, supposedly because it was a favourite picnic spot for the ladies from the castle. A golf course was opened here in 1850 but abandoned before the end of the century. The Michael pit too has gone and improved paths and tree plantings hide all these considerable past activities. Where the official coastal path swings right to continue along the tideline it is more interesting to take the left fork which angles up and along below the beech wood to take us into **East Wemyss**.

Below this path there used to be the Glass Cave; the name dating to seventeenth-century glassmaking. In 1901 the cave collapsed due to the workings of the Michael and was filled with *redd* (pit waste). In 1929 ground below a boiler in the pit cracked and a new cave was discovered below. (A piece of graffiti was dated 1690!) Archaeologists were given a grudged period to investigate before the cave was filled with concrete. A cup and ring mark and a hunting scene with an elk was noted; elk, extinct before the time of Christ, gives rise to some interesting speculation about dating the artwork. The Michael closed in 1967 after a disastrous fire that cost nine lives. The area of the site has now been landscaped and lies below. Looking ahead Buckhaven is clear, with arms of cranes behind and Largo Law on the skyline.

Memorial to the Michael disaster

We turn left along Randolph Street, one of the parallel 'rows' of what were miners' cottages, to reach the main road where we turn right. St Mary's Terrace is marked by a monument to the Michael disaster in the shape of a miniature winding tower. Keep along the A955 to a bus stop/wee shop labelled the Carshed, which, between 1906 and 1932, it was; on the tramcar line between Kirkcaldy's Gallatown and Leven. Continuing, on the landward side note two identical houses with the bowling green between. These were built for retired miners. I'm sure the mottoes were commented on: 'Put your trust in the Lord' (Wemyss?) and 'God helps those who work' (for Lord Wemyss?). The big red parish church is built of sandstone which came from North Yorkshire.

A few minutes more along the main road and we come to the big, bold Victorian Primary School/Library building on the seaward side. The Wemyss Environmental Centre is housed in the basement and has displays on the Wemyss Caves. During school hours, by appointment, one of the custodians will be happy to open the centre. Ring in advance: 01592-266361.

Follow down School Wynd which swings right and, where posts give only a pedestrian continuation, there is a plaque on the wall of what was an old toilet–about which more later. We come out to Sir Jimmy Shand Court (the *maestro* was born here; 1908) with the old church and war memorial ahead.

The war memorial is set in what were the original gates of the earlier parish churchyard and has a tiny figure of a soldier on top. St Mary's-by-the-sea is on a site dating back to the twelfth century and closed in 1976. Part of the building is now a private house. Most of the stones have weathered badly, but one, 1646, is very early, a 1761 stone has all the Ns incised in mirror image while many fisher feuars from Buckhaven have anchors portrayed. There's

Wemyss War Memorial

also a clear gun and powderhorn (hammerman) stone and one with a plough, which also has graceful calligraphy.

Follow Main Street seawards, then, beyond Weavers Court, it becomes East Brae and swings up steeply by a chunky building which was once a famous brewery. Go up the brae and in to the huge cemetery by a gate on the right. There is a Rennie Mackintosh designed memorial of no great quality, but it is the dangers of mining and sea–and war–that cry out from the stones. A white cherub marks the grave of 15-year-old Michael (Mickey) Brown, who was 'done to death' in 1909. He had been sent to Buckhaven by tram for the wages of the linen factory (its successor still exists down on the shore) and was waylaid and murdered by Alexander Edminstone, an unemployed miner, in the School Wynd lavatory on the way back. Edminstone disappeared with the money. There was a tremendous hue and cry but, through a poster in

Manchester, he was apprehended and brought back to Fife, crowds greeting his arrival and the press avidly printing his mother's letters to him in Perth prison where he was executed, the last prisoner to be hanged in that place. A recent booklet tells the horrific story fully: D.J. Currie: *Dark Skies Over School Wynd* (1998).

Return to the East Brae and down to the foreshore. A century ago this beach had sands, but now suffers serious erosion. Many miners built and raced small boats but fishing was never possible. George Moodie, captain of the *Cutty Sark*, was an East Wemyss chiel.

Michael Brown's grave

Turning along on our eastward way we come to a set of boards explaining the **Wemyss Caves** which lie ahead. (The boards are on setts in a pattern of the 'dumbell' symbol, such as is seen in Jonathan's Cave.) The caves only came to public knowledge in 1865 when symbols matching those of better known Pictish stones were recognised. The last decade has seen a great deal of storm damage with a lot of erosion threatening the caves. Pictures last century show a doocot which would now be 80 metres out in the sea. Human vandalism and neglect is a sadder element in much being lost. The inner doo cave collapsed when guns, sited above, were fired in W.W.I., though this may be a blessing yet with symbols of the swimming elephant (a Pictish beast), Z-rod and so on preserved undamaged on the walls. The caves at present are *very* dangerous and are best appreciated from one of the guidebooks available. They contain more prehistoric cave art than the rest of the country combined.

The Court Cave comes first, so named as baronial courts may have been held there. Pillars erected in the 1930s failed to stop a major roof collapse in 1970. Cup marks predate the Picts even. One drawing is popularly called Thor and the Sacred Goat. Doo Cave is next, recognisable from the surviving nest boxes on the wall. There's an inner cave, as mentioned, and mud flowing from it is building up to obscure some of the nest boxes. A 1945 storm took away the brick wall across the cave mouth which is the safest to enter.

Beyond the Doo Cave the official coastal path climbs very steeply up the bank to run along between a cemetery and the remains of Macduff Castle, then joins a gritty road onwards for Buckhaven, but this misses out the most interesting caves and it is worth keeping along the shore to see them. Something like £5 million has been spent on the sea defences for Dysart, West and East Wemyss, so one hopes access may be sure and safe eventually. We can only marvel at the awesome destructive power of the sea. Everything outwith a wall has gone and, inside that barrier, an old sewage pipe lies smashed among the boulders. The grills were placed on Jonathan's Cave following vandals setting fire to a car inside the cave, which flaked off several irreplaceable carvings; now the grill has been vandalised and graffiti endangers the walls. It seems extraordinary that so little has been done to protect this unique site.

'Thor and the Sacred Goat' in the Court Cave

The remains of Macduff Castle

Once across the rough going (or walking the sea wall) one comes to a grassy bay with Macduff's Castle above– and several caves below, including the once-famous Well Cave where Celtic Samhain (New Year) festivities gave way to Hansel Monday torchlight processions. Rockfalls make access both dangerous and irresponsible. A passage supposedly led up to the castle.

Macduff's Castle can be visited by a path from the grassy bay, but it has little interest beyond a stairway down to a cellar, lit by a gun loop. The exterior stonework is honeycombed by weathering. Old pictures show two towers, but the council blew one up in 1967 'for safety'. The castle is connected with the Thane of Fife who slew Macbeth. He had escaped along the coast to cross the ferry to North Berwick and refuge in England, but a castle then would have been constructed of wood. Edward I had a later castle burnt. The Wemyss family bought the castle back into the family in 1630 but let it go to ruin as they resided in Wemyss Castle. The plant Alexanders grows here, as at many castles; it was a sort of mediaeval celery.

If visiting the castle, descend again to the green bay. Continuing, one comes to the best of the caves, Jonathan's, said to be named from a one-time resident nailmaker. In 1988 the sea cut back 6m. to threaten the cave which is safe enough to enter. All but one of the carvings are on the west wall, the one being far back on the east side and showing the earliest delineation of a ship in Scotland. A graceful swan has given speculation that the Wemyss symbol as well as the Wemyss name (Gaelic for cave) came from here. A boar, fish, bull and various symbols are made out. In 1991 the Royal Museum took casts of everything possible.

Just round the next corner is Sloping Cave but it will only be reached by a narrow path and teetering on boulders and then one will have to come back the same way. Sloping Cave is now easier to enter due to the erosion. There is one carved symbol (left) and several holdfasts for tethering animals. The cave goes in far enough really to need a torch, and blocks on the floor give warning of the unstable roof. Other caves lie further along but are not worth visiting at present. White Cave is a bit of a mystery too. A small hole may be a way in, but excavation would be needed to investigate properly. Myth blows it up to huge dimensions (a passage to Kennoway!). Masonry on the shore is from old gas works, and Gasworks Cave is the last. A 1959 rockfall litters the interior where there was a prehistoric quern. Holdfasts line the east wall. Professor Simpson (of chloroform fame) and Dewar (thermos flask inventor) made the first exploration. Walking back past Jonathan's Cave, head up the track inland which climbs steeply, then crosses fields to reach the gritty grey track mentioned earlier. Turn right; soon the track ends and the continuation, all the way to **Buckhaven**, is a red, gritty path which follows the one-time tramway. Where the view opens out the fields below have had several bad landslips in the past, gaps opening large enough to swallow a tractor. Keep to the red path up some steps to continue round the bay. Inland the Rosie pit once stood–not a sign of it now. Nearing the town the path dips and turns sharp left, but it is pleasanter to go straight on up onto the green braes and walk round with open views. Below there are many huts on the site of a one-time busy harbour. Over the rooftops of Buckhaven are the skeletal cranes of a construction yard. Keep on to reach the furthest street.

Buckhaven is the anglicised name for what the locals still call Buckhynd, a *hynd* being a harbour arm, *buc* meaning to roar (both Norse words) and early maps sometimes had it as Hynde of Buck. The harbour has gone and so

have the sands that brought *pierrot* shows, bandstands
and Punch and Judy entertainment to Victorian children.
Daniel Defoe came spying in 1700 and called the place
'miserable', but he had been ripped-off and was unfor-
giving. A possible tradition is that shipwrecked
Dutchmen largely founded the town. Certainly its long
history as a fishing port made it a place apart. An 1866
directory lists 100 boats, but only 12 family names among
the owners. Weaving was also important, but inter-mar-
rying between the industries was rare for practical reasons
really: a weaver lass wouldn't be very good at baiting a
long line! A local mill supplied the yarn for the first trans-
atlantic cable.

   Walk along the end street (Viewforth, the only sign visible, but it is actually Randolph Street). Much of Buckhaven
was cleared in the sixties, with some hideous flat-roofed
boxes erected. Modern developments are more attractive.
The big frontage is the old Co-op building, and on the
corner when the main road is reached stand the Parish
church (St David's) and the Royal Bank of Scotland, the
one where the hapless boy Brown drew the wages that
led to his being murdered. The former church, St
Andrew's (next to St David's) once stood in St Andrews,
but was bought at a knock-down price and shipped, stone
by stone, to Buckhynd in 1872.

   We walk on, an hour or two of urban landscape which
can't be avoided but is not devoid of interest. On the right
the library houses an interesting small museum upstairs,
open during library hours. On the left the Primary School
still occupies an attractive 1915 building. It is worth going down the street opposite a short distance to see over
into the huge oil-rig construction yard. The site is on the
old Wellesley colliery, which closed in 1967, and this huge
sprawl of *redd* (waste) actually has buried the one-time
Links of Buckhaven hamlet. The *redd* eventually spilled
into the sea. In the sixties I can recall sea coal being col-
lected off Buckhaven beach, and black tidelines still
appear after storms as far west as Seafield.

   At the roundabout turn right along Wellesley Road.
This is now Denbeath, though there is no rural break between Buckhaven and Leven. Wellesley is from another
Wemyss family member, wife of Randolph. A certain
paternalistic philanthropy went with their exploitation

of the populace, and the still attractive hospital building is a high mark. Note the Wemyss swan on a gable wall plaque. The clock hands represent a miner's pick and shovel. The house next door, built for a doctor, is also a pleasing period piece.

When Wellesley Road bends we are right above the construction yard. A car park allows a view down into the works. The scale is impressive. The platforms ('men made monsters of the deep') are constructed on their sides and only turned upright once in the sea. Heading on, the next interest is on the landward side: a row of houses in the Wemyss style with red roofs and outside stairs. (Several similar rows lie behind.) The White Swan Hotel is a listed building marking the change from Denbeath, a 'new town' before its time, and Methil, which has a sadder look about it. Walk on to reach the small Memorial Park and skirt its seaward edge then to drop down into **Lower Methil**. The local war memorial has the figure of a kilted soldier, and lists 337 names. Ex-servicemen raised funds to stock the library opposite, opened in 1935. The trees were planted by all the local schools to celebrate the 1937 Coronation.

Turn left at the foot of the brae and at the Lower Methil sign walk straight on, on the High Street, rather than swinging right along by the largely silent docks. At one time (1904) 6½ million tons of coal was shipped from the Methil docks. Nothing has really replaced the mining and Methil has had a tough time for a long time. The building on the corner (red sandstone) has a weathervane of a horse. The brae here was once a mine tramway (as at Dalgety Bay). Methil was linked to Thornton by railway from 1887 till 1966 and there was also a Wemyss Private Railway, and the tramcars. Tracks, stations and the score of mines they served have all disappeared now.

The High Street of Lower Methil is 'penny plain' but you can amuse yourself by looking at house names to find the most pretentious. St Andrew's Square, set back on the right, is an attractive 1930s development which replaced slum housing. Further on, right, the old post office building (red sandstone again) houses the interesting new Methil Heritage Centre (Museum of Levenmouth); worth a visit and maybe a cup of tea. A plaque on the wall has a rare monogram–of Edward VIII.

The road comes to a junction; turn left, on Dubbieside, to pass an entrance to the docks, industrial estate and the home of East Fife Football Club. We reach **Leven** over the Bawbee Bridge. (A bawbee is an old Scots halfpenny.) The present bridge replaced an older one and, costing £200,000 in 1957, was the biggest bridge project since the war.

From the bridge there is a seaward view of a dominant power station which was specially built in the sixties to gob-

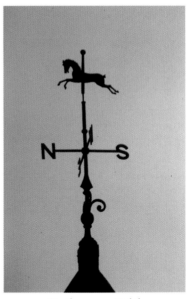

Weather vane, Methil

ble up the slurry, waste still being produced from active pits. Now the mining has gone and so have all the bings and waste across the county (which looks so green and tidy as a result) so its future is doubtful. With the disappearance of Edinburgh's sludge boat *Gardyloo* it was perhaps hoped to use that waste! The site was chosen because a plentiful supply of water is needed. The outflow water was warm and in winter appreciative swans and ducks gathered by the score. At present the site is 'mothballed'.

Leven had an active harbour at one time, all under the bus station or swimming pool complex area. Coal, linen, whisky, iron, potatoes and bone dust were the main exports. Methil Docks basically killed off Leven as a harbour. The Levenmouth pool is the pink building, one that was in at the start of such complexes with saunas, sports halls, café, etc., as well as the pool (open till 2200). A pedestrian crossing leads to the bus station and pedestrianised High Street, the main shopping centre for the urban miles we've walked. Leven will mark a break on our route. Most B&Bs are on the promenade.

A few comments on what to see. Leave the Shorehead bus station over on the right, South Street, which leads to

Rusticated quoins in Leven

a big car parking area. Turn right, into Seagate, to see
two remnants of a one time extensive use of shells, col-
oured glass, bits of broken pottery etc., in decorating
houses and gardens. Return to walk along the car parking area past the attractive 1874 Grey People's Institute
building (now housing a Job Centre and police station).
The name is from the original benefactor. The building
and cottages along Viewforth beyond have the typical
Fife 'rusticated quoins'–alternating long and short
dressed stones at corners and around the windows, often in contrasting colours or the darker being the local
whin stone. Turn left up School Lane to the other end of
the pedestrianised High Street (the main shopping/eat-
ing options are here if wanted). Up on the brick building
of the 1887 Co-op building (now the Library) there is a
plaque showing a skep with bees flying about. Along,
right, a 1935 version by the clock forgot to add the bees!
Those fascinated by cemeteries may want to continue
along Durie Street, otherwise that is really Leven explored. The continuation will be along the
Promenade–back down School Lane. (Leven has a Promenade, Kirkcaldy an Esplanade!)

Scoonie cemetery on the other hand repays a visit. This
means a ten minute walk on inland, Durie Street becom-
ing Scoonie Road and leading to a roundabout with the
graveyard to the right, above Scoonie Brae. Facing it is
Letham Glen, an attractive recreational park and animal

centre with burnside paths. (Described in Walk 12 of my *25 Walks: Fife* book, where a circuit is made to take in Silverburn as well.)

On the way back in to Leven note the number of church buildings. As a nation the Scots often tended to the zealously schismatic, and it would take a book to even outline their history. Look out for Carberry House on the left and go in to see the rare multi-faceted sundial in front of it. Drummond Castle, near Crieff, has the only other like it. Till 1767 it was Leven's mercat cross, was lost, found in a wall and eventually moved here for its own safety.

If this proves too long a day there are a few B&Bs on the route and buses also ply regularly between Kirkcaldy and Leven.

70

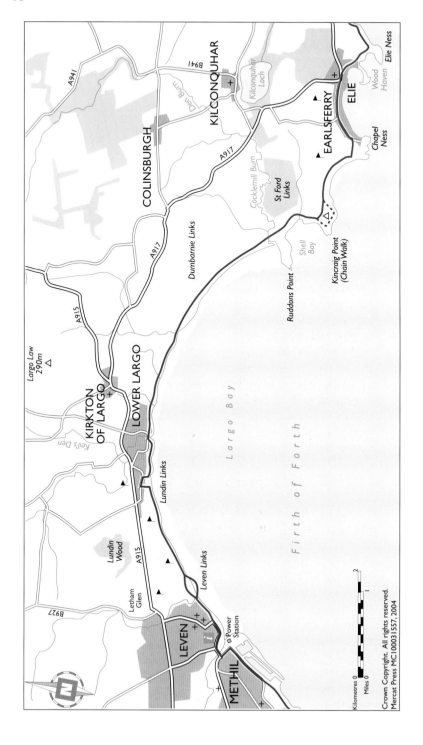

V
Largo Bay (Leven to Elie)
O.S. 59

This covers the most rural section of the estuary part of
the walk, then comes the interest of the East Neuk towns
and, to end, quite the hardest and longest empty miles
along what is often, rightly, called the 'Cold Coast'. Today's walking is easy, but it is worth carrying supplies,
especially liquid; there are not many watering holes on
the way round **Largo Bay.**

The walk is most easily picked up again on the Leven
promenade. Heading east again there is a path along by
the shore, or one can stay on the road for a while. Note the
Festival garden on the left with a monument commemorating the Polish Parachute Brigade who were based and
trained locally during the last war, and the end building,
in bold red brick, 1894 on gully boxes, a crest on the gable
and a text 'What holes wins' pointing to the 1820 founding of the Leven Golfing Society. The East Neuk is a
breeding ground of golf courses. Inland, beyond the bowling green, is the Leven Thistle Golf Club, with whom the
links are shared. Inland again is the municipal Scoonie
golf course, and, marching eastwards, Lundin golf course
(designed by James Braid). The road leads to the Leven
Beach Holiday Park (where camping is possible) and
there is a café. It can be passed on the landward side if
there is a high tide to frustrate walking along the beach.

Not far along there is a burn, the boundary between
the Leven and Lundin courses. Once a year a golf match
between the two is held over half of each course, out and
back, with a good social interval in the appropriate clubhouse at the halfway stage. The boundary is more
precisely the Mile Dyke, and if this is followed inland, a
five minute walk, **Silverburn** is reached, an estate in local
hands offering woodland walks (giant redwoods!), an attractive walled garden and picnic area. An amalgamation
of estates took the name Silverburn in 1854 when David
Russell established a flax industry, long gone, and planted
many exotic trees, now magnificent in their maturity.
Return by the Mile Dyke (the iron steps are a viewing

point for golfers) and continue on round the bay, the view now dominated by Largo Law.

This could be climbed from Lower Largo (see Appendix 2). The hill (*law* is a common Scots word for hill) is the local weatherman: 'When Largo Law puts on its cowl/ Look out for wind and weather foul'. The coast is more windy than wet–another good reason for walking the Fife coast.

One can walk along either on shore or dunes, but nearing Lundin Links, at a burn, one has either to go along the sands or turn inland across the golf course to follow its inland perimeter round to the clubhouse car park. Straight along on the crest of the dunes lands one in the clubhouse (doghouse?). The beach is simpler and shorter and, beyond the clubhouse, a path leads on clearly. The inland route soon drops down to join this, a children's play area is passed, then a track runs behind seaside houses to reach the road coming down from Lundin Links to Lower Largo.

Turn right to reach the old harbour/small estuary of **Lower Largo** dominated by the defunct viaduct of the Fife Coast railway, one of Beeching's closures in the sixties. The Railway Inn, a shop and Crusoe Hotel cluster round the mouth of the Keil Burn and can offer refreshments. Walk the twisting Main Street through the long village. A break on the right is the Orra, left, a road heads up to the A915 and then, set back a bit, left, is the town's

Lower Largo

main claim to fame, the statue on one of a cottage row.

'Robinson Crusoe' it is often called, but the figure, strictly speaking, is Alexander Selkirk, the prototype for Defoe's fictional character. Selkirk was born here in 1676 (in an earlier house) and was a bit of a wild lad who eventually went off to sea. He must have been a capable seaman for he was sailing-master of the ill-fated *Cinque Ports*, a ship where captain and crew (particularly Selkirk) were at daggers drawn.

Statue of Alexander Selkirk, Lower Largo

Selkirk asked to be put ashore on Juan Fernandez, off the South American Pacific coast, rather than continue on what he considered a leaky death trap. He took only a few supplies, for it was an island used for watering ships. He was there for over four years. The *Cinque Ports* sank soon after leaving him, the few captured survivors spending longer years in gaol than Selkirk did on his island.

When the road makes the right-angled turn seawards, take the footpath which goes straight on through to a car park, the site of an old drying green. (The house making this road diversion was once a net factory.) There are toilets and information boards and, at the landward side, steps go up, indicating the official coastal path which takes the dull, easy option of the old railway track. This is only worth following at the highest of tides, hidden behind the dunes as it runs, and half way along the bay it comes down to the shore again anyway. More interest will be found walking on through the last stretch of Lower Largo, where the road is often banded with wind-blown sand. This area is Temple, possibly a reference back to the Knights Templar.

On the left a signpost indicates the Serpentine Walk to

In Largo Bay

Upper Largo which is the route to follow if aiming to climb Largo Law (see Appendix 2). At the final turning spot of the road there are steps up onto the old railway line too, but it is more satisfying to wander the extensive sands if the tide allows. Paths wander along the dunes as well. A wedge of dunes in the middle of the bay is the SWT Dumbarnie Links Wildlife Reserve. Oil rigs are often anchored offshore.

Skylarks may be reeling overhead and there's a spaciousness unusual on the coast. The estuary has widened too, with the Lammermuirs rather than Edinburgh's Pentlands across its waters. Eider, scoter and long-tailed ducks may be seen. Land snail shells (often at thrushes' 'anvils') are colourfully banded. Old wartime defences and anti-tank blocks are slowly being swallowed by the dunes and there are plenty of rabbit burrows. The bay ends at the Cocklemill Burn and Ruddons Point.

The salt marsh here has a summer spread of sea aster and a backing of giant hogweed. One of the interests of the Fife coast is the huge range of shrubs and flowers to be found along the way. Among those found in wetter parts, see if you can spot kingcups, scurvy grass, butterbur, forget-me-not, woundwort, primrose, marsh lousewort, yellow flag (iris), dog's mercury, balsam, ragged robin, marsh cinquefoil, knotgrass, meadowsweet, marsh pennywort, sea mayweed, purging flax, sea milkwort, amphibious bistort, marsh felwort, sea spurrey,

wormwood, water dropwort, golden saxifrage, watercress, bogbean, various orache, thistle, chickweed,
willowherb, dock, sundew, orchids and violet species,
quite apart from grasses, reeds and rushes and what flour-
ishes *in* water, salt, brackish or fresh. Oddly, right next to
these areas, rocky places can be bright with plants de-
manding drier quarters: thrift, tormentil, wild strawberry,
kidney vetch, coltsfoot, thyme, bedstraw, stonecrops,
Scots bluebell, eyebright, valerian, ivy, travellers' joy,
gorse, silverweed, sea plantain, burnet rose, restharrow,
rock rose, cowslip, poppy and the like. Some areas seem
to welcome the barbed wire brigade of blackthorn, brambles, sweetbriar (and nettles) while the grassier slopes
can be colourful with campions, knapweeds, ox-eyed
daisy, yellow bedstraw, yarrow, scabious, agrimony,
cranesbills, comfrey, ragwort, bindweed, hawkbits,
Alexanders and various umbellifers. There's also yellow
rattle, viper's bugloss, hawkbits, buttercups, celandine,
daisy and dandelion, bracken in some places, elder and
various garden escapes. Both primrose and wild hyacinth
(the English bluebell) seem to cross habitat boundaries
at will, but I've seen snowdrops at the Kenly Burn in
flower *below* the level of a seaweed tidemark!

The **Cocklemill Burn** used to be quite a problem, often requiring a paddle or a diversion well upstream. A
millennium present was its bridging, though there may
be times when you'll paddle along the bridge, judging
by seaweed caught on the structure. There are two sturdy
bridges, in fact, well signposted at present, and leading
on to a track along the edge of the Shell Bay Caravan
Park (where camping is possible). At the start of last century a couple out walking discovered a prehistoric
'midden', with items like decorated combs, a bone pin, a
spindle whorl, a bone cup and remains of ox, sheep, pig,
rabbit, red and roe deer, dog and fox and also stones,
which were heated and dropped into water to cook food.
Across Shell Bay, running out to the point, the distinctive
steps of 'raised beaches' will be observed. (A periodic
feature of the East Neuk to look out for.) These indicate
former sea-levels and tie in with the various ice ages. Turn
off the caravan park to regain the shore: a path runs between fields of rich soil and the shore.

Turning the point the path climbs the successive levels

of the raised beaches. For the second it breaks into steps
and, just before it swings left for the third steepening, a
barely noticed path breaks off, right, very steeply down
to shore level. This is the way to the Chain Walk, Scotland's unique *via ferrata*, which is described in Appendix
3. The path proper climbs steps again and then traverses
over the top of **Kincraig Hill**, 63m., another viewpoint
out of all proportion for its modest height. There are several wartime remains on the way and an observation post
down some steps. Below on the shore are some strangely
flat areas and ruler-straight dykes. There are two com-
munication masts on top. (The trig point is not quite on
the highest spot.) A path leads us on, past an obvious
gun emplacement, then, from another concrete post, angles down to **Earlsferry** links and **Elie** golf course. For
safety it is better to walk along the sands, themselves attractively warm in colour, and the rocks with beards of
green weed. At high tide keep to the path along the dunes.

Near the far end there is a sunken track (Sea Tangle
Road) coming down to the sands; turn up this (with care!),
then, after 130m., turn right along a fence to go round
Chapel Ness. Note how the trees have been planed by
the wind. A grassy track (where cowslips grow) leads
along outside the houses (built of dark whinstone) to open
up a view over the reef of East Vows to the Bass Rock.
The beacon didn't prevent a ship, *Vulcan*, running onto
the rocks in 1882 with its load of pig iron. But what was a
boat from Middlesborough to Grangemouth doing there
at all? The ruined gable is all that remains of an eleventh-
century pilgrim chapel, where pilgrims rested after their
ferry crossing from Dunbar en route to St Andrews. As
many as 10,000 a year made the hazardous crossing.
Macduff, thane of Fife, is thought to have built a chapel
in 1093 as an offering to the ferrymen who rowed him
over to safety after Macbeth had slaughtered his family
at his East Wemyss castle in 1054. The Reformation rather
killed off pilgrimages, and the easier, safer ferries at
Pettycur, Burntisland or Queensferry grew in importance.
Steamers once operated Leith-Elie-North Berwick, till
World War I brought their end.

Earlsferry has a hotch-potch but some pleasing architecture of trim calm. Walking along the High Street note
the fancy iron brackets holding the gutters, and the

Elie

graceful doorway beyond, at a 'no entry' sign for vehicles. The High Street goes on with no break past Williamsburgh and Liberty to **Elie** (they were separate burghs till 1929). The town hall (1872) has the clock tower with a sailing ship weather vane. The house opposite has a sundial with several faces on its west skew putt. A plaque by the town hall door commemorates James Braid, a local golfer, who won the Open *five times* in the years 1901-10. Polish forces are commemorated on a wall plaque. All along the coast broad Fife accents can belong to surnames like Matyssek or Peplinska, for many stayed on and married local lassies. 'Wynd' is a euphoric word for lane: Glovers Wynd, Castwell Wynd, Cadger's (Carrier's) Wynd and Cross Wynd are on our route, the last presumably once the mercat cross site. Two-way traffic resumes after Ferry Road.

After Liberty turn up Golf Club Lane, which leads up to the Elie Sports Club complex. The Pavilion Café by the tennis courts may be welcome. But the main interest is over to the left beyond the golf club house: a hut with a long tube rising from it. This is the starters' hut for Elie Golf Course, and because the first drive is blind, in 1966 they installed the periscope from a 1954 submarine *Excalibur* to see if the fairway ahead was free. *Excalibur* was an experimental submarine powered by hydrogen peroxide, an idea superseded by nuclear power. Some of the notices indicate golf as a last bastion of male chauvinism!

Return to the linear route which now becomes Links Place. An attractive modern development has a mural carving of a boat. In the past (and the nickname has been retained) this was jokingly called 'the Sahara Park', no doubt from sand perpetually blowing off the beach. The Post Office has an attractive sign. Turn down right thereafter into Fountain Road, which leads to South Street, the original High Street of the royal burgh where several ancient buildings survive. Gillespie House (left) has a 1682 lintel for Alex Gillespie and Christina Small. The doorway (the 'muckle yett') with a ruined sundial over it is the remains of a sawpit for timber imported from the Baltic. On the seaward side the Castle is fifteenth-century, the town house of the Gourlays, related to the Sharps, one of whom, the hated Archbishop, was murdered as he rode in his carriage to St Andrews.

Turn left up School Wynd to reach the main crossroads of Elie, as one could gather from the meeting of School Wynd, High Street, Bank Street and Park Place. The Victoria Hotel occupies one corner, opposite is the war memorial (looking like a gateway) while the churchyard entrance is along a bit, the old session house with odd finials. The baker on the corner sells *sair heids* (sore heads).

The church is quite dominant, built in the early seventeenth century, but the tower added in 1726. There are only three faces to the clock as, when installed in 1900, there was no town on the fourth side. When the clock

Elie Kirk

was renewed the workings went to Edinburgh, where they still drive the works of Princes Street's famous floral clock. The church is a typical T-shape, with the pulpit central and facing the laird's loft. A major addition, when the church united with the Wood Memorial Church, was the addition of their Burne-Jones windows.

The graveyard is mostly Victorian, but some earlier stones have been placed at the east end of the church (outside). One seems to be a skeleton, 'rolled up in a carpet', so all that shows are skull, stark ribs and feet. This commemorates a daughter of Turnbull of Bogmill (d.1650) whose large decorative slab also stands against the wall. The bull's head, turned aside, is a pun on the family name.

At a meeting of paths by the east porch is a stone inscribed to Charles Fox Cattanach, wife (*sic*) of James Smith, Ship Master... and James Smith her (*sic*) husband'. Apparently the minister mixed up names at the christening and the superstitious family insisted the girl went through life with her male Christian name. There used to be a 'lang grave' for a drowned sailor found on the shore with arms outstretched, and superstition forbade the breaking of the arms to fit a conventional grave. A sorry number of stones testify to the dangers of the sea. One accident happened in full view of family and friends when a boat was fishing between the harbour and the ferry chapel on an apparently calm day, only to be overturned by a squall. One widow gave birth to a girl a few days later and she was given her father's name, Andrew. One woman lost husband, brother and brother-in-law.

The masons building the church inserted a black stone as a safeguard against witches, a real horror, in Fife and the Lothians mainly, with an estimated 4,400 women burnt as witches between 1590 and 1680. It was hardly a peaceful century, nor the time perhaps to be erecting a church. When the English Civil War broke out in England, Scott of Ardross, the laird, went off to support King Charles while the Scots parliament and church opposed him. The Elie minister went south too, so was opposing his own patron. Scott was captured at the Battle of Worcester and lost his estates. The Anstruthers became the new owners, having played their war games a bit more successfully. Balcaskie House, inland, is still in the Anstruther family.

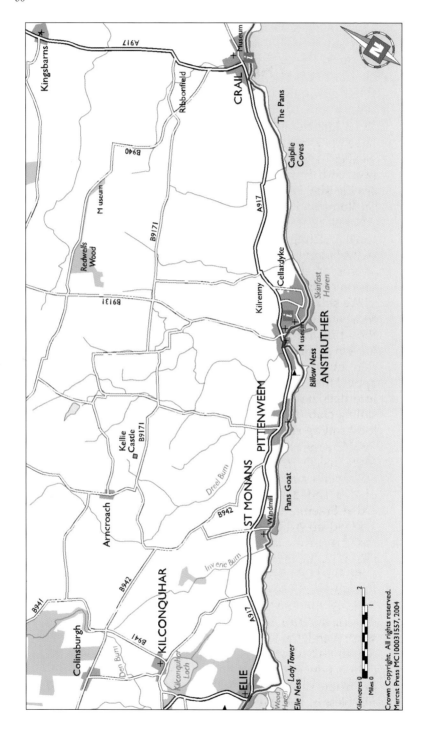

VI
The East Neuk
O.S. 59

From Elie Ness (Point) back to Pettycur (Kinghorn) we have really been coasting round a huge bay made up of smaller bays. The East Neuk has a much more open aspect, with the feeling of sea rather than estuary. Out in the sea the May Island (see Appendix 4) catches the eye with the 'lump and cone' of Bass Rock and North Berwick Law on the far shore. As much time can vanish exploring the towns, 'strung like pearls', as can walking the thread of paths linking them; one can stop, start and use transport at will rather than being strictly programmed by my division of the route.

We still have some of **Elie** to view as we set off. Continue along the High Street past the garden (Toll Green), then turn right down to the sea. The curving road is known as the Toft. Admiralty Lane, left, is our continuation, but a walk out along the 1586 harbour arm may appeal first. The big building is the Granary, now turned into flats, beyond the clutter of watersports centre and sailing club. There a viewpoint indicator on a knoll. The local sailing club's first Hon. Commodore was Admiral Sir William James, who is known much better as the boy in the painting, 'Bubbles', used in Pears Soap advertising. Their first boat was called *Bubbles*. The ill-fated Earl of Mar landed at Elie before going on to raise the standard at Braemar to start the 1715 Jacobite rebellion.

Head up Admiralty Lane and turn right to reach the parking/picnic area on the bay of Wood Haven. At the far end, right, there is a gate which commences the coastal path to St Monans. Wood Haven is more often called Ruby Bay (the rubies were garnets) and ends at a prow overlooking the 1908 lighthouse: a pair of battlemented towers, one square, one round, which are actually on a small island. David Stevenson supervised this light's erection in 1908. Carbide gas lighting has long gone and the light is now automatic. A Russian schooner *Jupiter*, sailing from Alloa to Riga with coal, 'took the ground' off Elie Ness in 1897. Five crew were saved by breeches buoy, but the mate and captain refused to leave their doomed ship. A month later a salvage lighter, *Grangemouth*, was anchored over the sunken schooner and, in only a force 7, went ashore too and now lies alongside *Jupiter*.

The grassy path swings east towards an obvious tower, the Lady Tower, built c.1760 and named after Lady Janet Anstruther, 'a coquette and a beauty' according to Carlyle, who liked to swim in the sea and had a tower and grotto changing room below built to satisfy her whim. A bellman was sent through the town to warn plebs to keep away. The tower is still a good viewpoint.

Our path heads along marram-held dunes above the typical warm-coloured sands. Elie House lies inland and the trees there are beginning to take on that wind-planed appearance that becomes more and more obvious as we head east till trees themselves almost disappear. By Ardross there is only just room to squeeze in the A917 road, old railway line and path. Where a track heads inland under a bridge, note the basalt dyke that runs down the shore like a man-made wall. The path wiggles on and the rock is suddenly tawny sandstone, so the next stretch of bay has 'silver sands' as against the 'golden sands' of the East Links back the way. At low tide the ragged reefs reach out to sea one after the other (volcanic rock, more resistant than the sedimentary between). From a small point immediately below, slabs with the marks of fossilised ripple marks can be seen. A few feet above them there's a small coal seam.

The path wends through ruinous Ardross Castle, erected in 1370 by Sir William Dishington when sheriff of Fife. He married a sister of Robert the Bruce. From the castle an eighteenth-century rectangular lectern-style doocot can be seen near the main road. Our path leads down, passing a filled-in railway bridge, to a bay where proper embanking has been made to protect the line. The views are good, both ahead and back to the Lady Tower.

Newark Castle is approached by steps up the cliff which has remnants of masonry clinging to it. There's a post on the shore and a notice warns that if the sea is above it an alternative route on from the castle may be advisable. This heads directly inland to a track, then, before a house, turns right to follow a long field edge to an isolated one-time railway bridge with a small span over

The coast at Ardross

the Inweary (St Monans) Burn and a larger arch for a path to the A917. Follow the burn down to the sea at St Monans Church to join the *voie normale*.

Newark Castle is a gaunt spectacle, its local sandstone badly weathered, more impressive for its setting than its architectural interest. Little remains apart from the four walls and a row of vaulted cells. Last century Sir Robert Lorimer produced a grand plan for restoring the castle for Sir William Burrell, the shipping magnate. Had this gone ahead the Burrell Collection could well have been here! The castle was bought by Fifer David Leslie in 1649, and it was from this building he took his title, Earl of Newark, the reward for finally defeating 'the great Montrose' at the Battle of Philiphaugh (where prisoners were massacred afterwards in the other Newark Castle). Just beyond the castle is its sixteenth-century beehive doocot, weathered, but complete, perched on a prow above the sea, the Isle of May beyond. The interior has an impressive depth of pigeon droppings–and dead birds. A gate by the doocot leads us on, swooping downwards, then along towards the church. Just short of it we are diverted down some steps to walk along the foot of an embankment to reach the inlet with a slip and the Inweary Burn. This rather fatuous diversion is the cause of the long inland high tide option, whereas in the past one just stepped over the cemetery wall to reach the church, which should be visited.

St Monans often appears, less accurately, as St
Monance. Before the cult of the saint it was Inverie or
Inweary. The church dates back to *c*.1265 and stands by
the Inweary (St Monans) Burn. The entrance is at the side
by the Honest Man's grave, a flat slab dated 1605 and
appropriately inscribed round the rim. We enter by a door
(with a posthole) into what is the original south transept,
and the pulpit and communion table are at the crossing,
facing the chancel–so in pre-Reformation days the altar
would be at the far end. Surprisingly, sacramental niches,
piscina and sedila have survived. An older model ship
(eighteenth-century) and one of a fishing boat hang in
the church, whitewashed and plain as the interior is. Display boards give plenty of information.

David II was largely responsible for rebuilding the
church in 1346, Dishington, the laird, picking up the bill.
Legends conflict as to why the king undertook this work:
one says he was hit by two arrows at the Battle of Neville's
Cross and at St Monan's shrine one of the shafts 'leapt
out of the wound', the other says he was crossing the
Forth to Ardross Castle, was caught in a storm, and made
the vow to build a church if saved. The English burnt the
church in 1544, but in 1646 it was made the local parish
church. In the 1950s it had to be rescued from decay and
heavy-handed Victorian alterations. It has always been a
sea-mark but, oddly, there is no weathercock.

The ragged formation offshore is named the Boiling

St Monan's Church

Cauldron, and can echo and boom dramatically in the surf. Legend says witches were thrown into the sea to gain a good catch. Fishermen have always been both godly and superstitious. No boat would leave a Fife port if a pig, a cat, a minister or a female was encountered when preparing for sea. Certain words also were never to be uttered, including names with double consonants, such as Watt, Ross, Marr. Any potential fear was allayed by touching iron (not wood).

John Paul Jones keeps appearing. He was a Kirkcudbright youth who proved a brilliant seaman and became one of new America's first heroes. In British history books of course he is a villain. When he made his raid on the Forth he kidnapped a St Monans man as pilot, but he proved so ineffective he had to be replaced. His most famous quote was in a 1799 battle when his ship was sinking under him and he was hailed about surrendering. He shouted back, 'I have not yet begun to fight'. His remit, as an American captain, was to 'distress' the enemy, which he did with élan.

Leaving St Monan's churchyard, cross the burn and go right of the house opposite. A narrow footpath climbs up by several gardens to come out on a road (Braehead) from which take the right fork to drop down again. As the road swings left the harbour comes into view. Continue along attractive West Shore, reaching the harbour at a big slip where some shipbuilding continues. The huge shed is a relic of Millers' shipyard, Scotland's oldest, which closed in 1993. The two outer harbour arms were built by the Stevenson family, the central pier was assisted by nationwide donations to help local poverty. Mid Shore leads

Summer in the East Neuk

to the eastern side of the harbour, with several wynds leading off into quite a maze of period houses, with fore-stairs, crowstep gables, pantiles, harled walls and so on, which would repay a wander. The post office and neighbouring buildings are more NTS restorations. Opposite the mine (where there's a collecting box) turn up Station Road then first right onto East Street to see a fine blend of old and new, showing what can be done ('imitation vernacular' indeed!). The street swings to Virgin Square.

Don't head off along East Shore, which would seem the obvious way on, but head up (along Forth Street) then first right, to Rose Street, really a narrow lane from which a path of red chips will take us on to Pittenweem. The **windmill** ahead is the main attraction *en route*. A path leads up to it once past the grassy recreational area and outdoor pool (opened in 1937 but no longer maintained). There's a children's picnic area below the windmill. The windmill pumped sea water up to the salt pans. In the eighteenth century Sir John Anstruther opened new coal pits for the salt pans, which were connected to Pittenweem by a waggonway. A major underground fire in 1794 caused a slump, and the salt pans were abandoned by 1823. You can still see the holding tank between tidelines and the cut where the water was piped up. Inland, the farm is called Coal Farm. As we continue, a stream rushing down is the chalybeate well of St Monans, so iron-impregnated that the fishermen washed their nets in its water to make them more durable.

Easy walking leads us on and, when the path forks, take the left branch, past an irony spring, to gain the prow above, where there's a shelter, benches, play area and car park. Down at sea level concrete arms indicate a bathing area dating back to before World War One. The pristine sandy nook may appeal. A dip right now? Skirt right from the shelter–and suddenly **Pittenweem** is in view. A row of houses (West Shore) rims a quiet bay, a corner few visitors see. There was once a gas works bang in the middle and the slip was probably to supply the works with coal. Houses must have found the sea wall little defence in big storms. The wall was tarred as a protection. Spur stones mark the opening past the last house–and we come to the wider Mid Shore.

A reef on the right makes an almost natural slip and is

Pittenweem

a good viewpoint. On the left the house with a pend (passage) is the Cooperage, an indication of its past use. Pittenweem's main use today is as the coast's home fishing port (a port was first mentioned in 1228), and the frequent KY registration stands for Kirkcaldy. Boat names are as varied and interesting as house names. The fish market stands over to the right at the harbour, protected by a long arm, the end of which (with a harbour light) is an unusual viewpoint for Pittenweem. Fife has fascinating place names and an anonymous rhyme suggests, 'Largo, Blebo, Dunino/ Into Europe seem to go,/ But plainly Scottish we may deem/ Auchtermuchty, Pittenweem.'

All the wynds deserve exploration but we will have to be selective. Cove Wynd (it should be Cave Wynd) lies up from the mine collection box and has the historical feature of St Fillan's Cave. Pittenweem appears on a charter of David I as Pit-ne-weme: *the place of the cave*. The cave is locked to prevent vandalism, but a key can be obtained at the Gingerbread Horse, 50m. along the High Street, left at the top of Cove Wynd. The church is right at the top of Cove Wynd and its key can be found at the chemists in Market Street, a bit further along the High Street. (Obviously only available during shop hours, and check on-site notices in case of a change. The Gingerbread Horse is also a tempting tearoom/craft shop.)

While fetching keys note the Kelly Lodging halfway along the High Street (landward side), once the town house of the Earls of Kellie, with corbelled turret and other sixteenth-century features. Walking back the church dominates the view, the tower looking very like the tolbooth it once was. Against the wall is the shaft of the mercat cross. The bell was cast in 1663 for 'Joran Puttensen's widow' and is Swedish. Just left of the gate into the churchyard, among the good selection of seventeenth-century table stones, is one with an anything but modest inscription (to David Binning *d.*1675).

Seaward of the church are the scant ruins of an Augustinian Priory where the monks based on the rather threatened May Island were granted a site near the already famous cave. St Fillan was a seventh-century missionary, so the cave, still laid out as a chapel, is one of Scotland's oldest religious sites. There's a well in the left inner chamber and a stair leads up to a chamber 10m. overhead in the Priory garden.

Having returned the keys, descend School Wynd (first wynd westwards) back to the harbour and walk towards the east end, where the much-photographed houses of the Gyles (restored by NTS) look on the outer harbour. *The Winter Guest* film (starring Emma Thomson) made use of the Gyles and the Pittenweem scenery generally. The three-storey house is a sea captain's home of 1626.

The seventeenth century was an intolerant century, and as late as 1705 three women died and many others were tortured on a witchcraft charge based on the accusations of a teenager. One of the three died after five months of torture and incarceration, another starved to death in her cell, the third escaped only to be caught and lynched by a mob who dragged her to the harbour and swung her over the water to be stoned, then crushed her under a door over which a horse and cart were driven back and forth.

Pittenweem has an annual Arts Festival each August, when over 40 sites (from Kelly Lodging to rooms in houses) have exhibitions. Gardens are also open and cafés appear in back gardens and terraces over the sea. Of its kind it is one of the happiest festivals. Too far inland if afoot, but worth visiting, is the NTS Kellie Castle and Garden, restored by Sir Robert Lorimer last century. The garden is a noted organic showpiece.

But to push on eastwards; from the Gyles head up Abbey Wall Road and when the brae swings left, take a

The Gyles, Pittenweem

wall opening, right, to go through a play area and off along the cliff top behind a housing scheme. The strong diagonal strata out to sea is, ominously, the Break Boats. The cliff is badly eroded; at several places today we walk on the brink or see older paths fenced off for safety. Down to the shore again, follow the edge of Anstruther golf course, the only real gap between the towns. Anstruther ('Ainster' locally) is an incorporation of four old royal burghs: Anstruther Wester and Easter, Cellardyke and

Kilrenny–a link-up rather contrasting with Buckhaven, Denbeath, Methil and Leven. There is not much to see along the way: the concrete box is an old anti-aircraft gun site, there's a lookout post (closed) and another forgotten rock bathing pool at Billow Ness. In 1935 a coal boat went aground offshore and swimmers found amusement in swimming out to the stranded boat.

At the grassy point of Billow Ness we gain a good view to **Anstruther**. The offshore jut of rock (with a marker post) is Johnny Doo's Pulpit, but it has an entirely historical ecclesiastical connection for the young local lad, Thomas Chalmers, came here to practice his sermons. He was licensed to preach by St Andrews Presbytery at the age of 19, but then studied mathematics at Edinburgh before an appointment at St Andrews. He later became minister at Kilmany (Fife's), and Glasgow (first the Tron, then St John's) where his preaching drew large crowds and his work for the poor was outstanding. The century-old fight against patronage was coming to a head, and in 1843 Chalmers was a leader in the Disruption, when nearly half the Church of Scotland ministers walked out rather than tolerate the undemocratic and often misused system–an incredible act of faith and defiance, for the

Tideline houses of the East Neuk

ministers lost church, manse and salary at a stroke, and often had difficulty in establishing new churches, the landowners being anything but helpful. Congregations sometimes had to meet between the tidelines, and there was a floating church in the west.

The battlemented tower up on the golf course (above the swings) is the local war memorial. Nets protect walkers from golf balls, though, I suspect, these were erected to stop sliced drives ending in the sea. The course is 9 holes, in an attractive setting. Pass the club-house and turn right, keeping on and only turning left, into Crichton Street, to reach the A917. The popular Craw's Nest Hotel and several B & Bs lie left, on the Pittenweem road. We turn right to follow the High Street (of **Anstruther Wester**), passing the Dreel Tavern, where a plaque mentions one of the stories of the Guid Man o Ballengeich, as James V

Crossing the Dreel Burn, Anstruther

was called on his anonymous wanderings. There was no bridge over the Dreel Burn then and he was naturally carried over by a gaberlunzie (beggar) woman who, instead of the expected pittance, was paid in gold.

As the main road turns sharply to cross the Dreel Burn, note the seventeenth-century house on the corner, covered in seashells, the work of one Alex Batchelor last century. Buckie House (buckie in the loose sense of shell, not one species) has parts harled with shells, and the main front is highly decorative with a triple frieze of scallop shells at the top. Batchelor used to charge a penny to let people see his coffin, which was also decorated with shells.

Across the road is an obviously old church, now the parish church hall, while, beside it, on the Esplanade (the lane leading off seawards at the bad bend) is the eighteenth-century town hall. In the thirteenth century it is said an iron basket on top of the tower was lit as a beacon to guide shipping in to harbour. The weathervane is a salmon, and the church was dedicated in 1243 to St Nicholas, patron saint of the sea. The graveyard has superb sea views–and some interesting stones, including a very early one dated 1598 now set in the wall. The tablet next to it has good Biblical Scots on it (Yat is *yett*, a gate).

East, over the burn, is the historic Smugglers Inn. If the tide is well out, go down the Esplanade. If the tide is full, still go down the Esplanade but then come back and on to the Smugglers Inn. At low tide ancient stepping stones allow one to cross the mouth of the burn–hence the options.

The Esplanade (odd name, for it isn't) has several good buildings. A plaque at the start commemorates John Keay, a local lad who became captain of the *Ariel* and other clipper ships. The *Ariel* and *Taeping* (built for Captain Rodger of Cellardyke) took part in the most famous tea clippper race of all time in 1866. Both came in to the Thames (from Foochow in China) on the same tide! Several houses are visibly dated, and the wheatsheaf on an old cottage may point to its having been an inn. Steps lead down to the big stepping stones across the Dreel Burn to **Anstruther** itself.

Across the river once stood Dreel Castle, where Mary Queen of Scots slept and Charles II gave his hosts the backhanded compliment for his supper: 'Aye, no a bad bite for a craw's nest'. The row of houses (Castle Street) leads us to Shore Street, the heart of the Anstruthers.

If having to avoid the Dreel Burn and crossing by the A917, note the plaque on the bridge marking a 1795 re-building of the 1630 bridge. (There's also been an 1831 remodelling.) The Smugglers Inn is an old coaching inn, but the name no doubt is justified, and would be anywhere on this coast. Break off the High Street just past the inn with the Royal Hotel visible at the end of this lane. Off it (along Old Post Office Close) is the house where Chalmers was born, old long before then, with ships' masts and timbers used as roof beams. Turn right to gain Shore Street. Left is Tolbooth Wynd, but it lost the tolbooth in 1871 (the iron *yett* is at the Fisheries Museum). The big red sandstone building is the 1908 Murray Library (style: 'fussy Renaissance'); Murray was a local lad who made good trading with Australia. Across from here, not best sited by the bus stop, is the 1677 mercat cross. As at Pittenweem a walk out on the harbour arm gives a good view of the handsome town frontage. The light is the Chalmers Memorial Lighthouse, an 1880 gift, as was the first lifeboat in 1865, from a Cheltenham lady who never ever visited Anstruther. The Chalmers Memorial

Church steeple for long dominated the view to the town, and was a useful sea mark on this low, featureless coast. Vandals in 1991 set fire to the unused church which had to be demolished.

Though bigger than Pittenweem, Anstruther's eighteenth-century harbour is hardly used now, the crowded days pre-war long gone as fishing has declined. Robert Louis Stevenson lived here while his father was enlarging the harbour in 1860. At that time he was expected to follow the family business of lighthouse and harbour building, and had not yet made his break for literature. He was to apologise: 'Though I haunted the breakwater by day and even loved the place for the sake of the sunshine, the thrilling seaside air, the wash of the waves on the sea-face, the green glimmer of the divers' helmets far below, and the musical clinking of the masons, my one genuine preoccupation lay elsewhere, and my only industry was in the hours when I was not on duty'.

At the east end of Shore Street is the Scottish Fisheries Museum, a major attraction and one of the best. (The café may be welcome too.) The building is on St Ayles land which has recorded connections with the fishing industry in 1318. The laird of 'Anstroyir' then made over rights to Balmerino Abbey, including the erection of fishing booths and drying nets. A chapel was built in the fifteenth century, but the site has been 'recycled' several times over, including for its apt present use, opening in 1969. There is a wide range of exhibits and re-creations, a working wheelhouse, a collection of boats and much else. Allow plenty of time for a visit. There is also a Tourist Information Office next door.

Scottish Fisheries Museum, Anstruther

The Battle of Kilsyth in 1645 saw so many local men slain that it is blamed for a decline in East Neuk fortunes. In 1670 a storm devastated harbours and houses too, and the 1707 Union brought no benefit: in that year the Ainsters had 30 boats, in 1764 there were 5. Over-fishing (by both home and foreign boats) saw the herring industry die last century.

Just east of the museum, go through Whale Close to East Green, where there's a plaque to Captain John Smith, skipper of *Min* and *Lahloo* in the tea clipper days. He was drowned when his ship was lost with all hands off the Hebrides in 1874. The town's famous school, Waid Academy, was endowed by a Royal Navy officer, Andrew Waid (1736—1803). You can't escape sea connections in Anstruther. (Gifford notes the 1930 school extension, 'in polite harl and red brick', and the 1956 council's as 'aggressive concrete'.) Head back westwards to where East Green meets Haddfoot, a stey brae which justifies 'Hadd-the-feet!' (Watch your feet!) On it, left, there is some decoration owing its moulding to egg boxes. Behind gates lies a big house (Johnstone House) which was once the home of a Tahitian princess. She had married a Scots merchant, and when he died she married an employee, George Dairsie, who brought her 'home'. The house was bought by a son-in-law solicitor, and he added a ballroom for his fun-loving wife who, widowed, had to sell out to a half-sister. She'd cannily married a minister whose main reading was the *Financial Times,* and who made a fortune.

Scottish merchants often fell foul of the Inquisition in Spain and were imprisoned or burnt as heretics, so there was something of an about turn when the ships of the Spanish Armada came to grief. A party of 260 Spaniards from Medina's *El Gran Grifon* somehow made their way from the Northern Isles to Anstruther, much to the consternation of the people. James Melville, the redoubtable local minister, could speak Spanish and made his opinions plain but, nevertheless, Scottish folk succoured *any* in distress. The Spaniards were given hospitality until repatriated. This paid off, for later, when an Anstruther ship was seized in Spain and it came to the notice of Medina who rescued men and ship, and entertained the men, in return for their good turn at Anstruther. Melville's

Manse still exists. Local booklets on the area can be found at the Museum. We must push on.

Heading on from the Fisheries Museum we enter the lang toon of **Cellardyke,** which is so overshadowed by Anstruther to which it was attached in 1929. Keep along the shore road by the Sun Tavern, passing the two green leading lights and then swinging right. New houses, Harbour Lea, left, have been highly praised. The road swings inland, but we keep on along the road parallel to the sea all the way through Cellardyke. This is James Street (not mentioned initially) which runs along to Tolbooth Wynd, the original tolbooth replaced by the 1883 municipal building, against which is the surviving shaft of the 1642 mercat cross. Our shore road now becomes John Street, then George Street, where a plaque recalls an otherwise forgotten rhymester, 'Poetry Peter' (Smith). The open space of the harbour area comes as a contrast, but the harbour is barely used now. The older name was Skinfast Haven. An offshore reef is Cuttyskelly. Telford's fellow engineer, Joseph Mitchell, rebuilt an earlier harbour dating away back. In the mid-nineteenth century a small Greenland whaling company operated from here but lost out to bigger Dundee boats. A cod-liver-oil factory has also gone. Just past the end of the harbour a house called Taeping commemorates Captain Alexander Rodger, a local fisherman who became captain and then owner of several clippers, *Min, Lahloo* and *Taeping* among the more

Cellardyke Harbour

famous. (His fisherman father had died at the Burntisland drave–the annual herring fishing–in 1814.) One of his contemporaries was Walter Hughes who roamed many seas, ran opium from China to Siam till too risky, started a sheep-run the size of Fife in Australia, found copper, became the richest man in Australia, which bought respectability, so he retired with a knighthood. James Clavell take note.

The Braes and Town Green now flank to the inland side of us, on the right a row of tidily-restored houses; one, the Cooperage, has craft symbols carved on the corner. Barrel-making in 1833 employed 70 coopers, as an example of how big this trade once was. Cellardyke alone had 24 breweries. Cellardyke folk were no more thirsty than anywhere else; beer was simply the everyday drink in those days. Tea was the luxury (strange role-reversal). The stone on the corner shows the tools of this trade, which the tea clippers presumably helped to kill off. The Town Green was a gift from Captain Rodger.

Cellardyke rather peters out: there's a children's play area, the war memorial up on the Braes and another forgotten tidal pool before the final car park. (The rocks beyond the pool are the Cardinal's Steps, where the newly created prelate, Cardinal Beaton, went aboard his barge to travel to St Andrews in style.) The caravan park surrounds what was Kilrenny Mill. Kilrenny itself, only a hamlet, lies up on the A917 and we only glimpse a St Monan's-like spire as we walk on. The spire too was a good sea mark and, oddly, many fishermen lived up in Kilrenny. Cellardyke was often called Nether Kilrenny. We follow a track right by the shore, crossing the Kilrenny Burn by a bridge and passing fields given over to pig-rearing. **Caiplie** Farm (converted in flats) is unusual, being at shore level rather than up on a raised-beach level. There's an octagonal (pantiled) wheelhouse, another east coast feature. Fossil tree stumps can be found on the shore. The May Island shows its steepest profile and is at its nearest to shore. The twins of Bass and Law lie beyond.

A few fields on we come to the stark feature known as the Caiplie Coves, a sea-carving of caves on the 8m. raised beach, multi-hued and weathered into fantastic shapes. The main cave (Chapel Cave) has several incised crosses dating back to early Christian days, when missionaries

Caiplie Coves

such as Adrian may have lived here. The Covenanter
Peden once used its shelter, and early this century the
cave was taken over by 'Covey Jimmy', Jimmy Gilligan
from Aberdeen who served in the Boer War, Afghani-
stan and elsewhere, spoke French and Latin but, hating
city life, set up home here in 1910. The coast becomes
rougher. At the Millport Burn there are yellow flags and
celandine. Watercress may harbour sheeps' liver fluke and
the celery-like dropwort is best avoided–it was a popular mediaeval poison! A white cottage, tucked in a bay,
was a salmon bothy. Saltworks, dating back to c.1700,
explain the name, the Pans. Later there were brickworks,
some ruins of which remain. The walking is probably the
loneliest on the coast till now, and quite atmospheric some
find with the sweeping sea views. A pull up a prow brings
Crail into near view, and we dip down and then up again
to reach the historic town.

The shoreline is rough and impractical, so the path rises
up to go round the cliffs into **Crail**–and, doing so, gives
classic views down to the tiny, tidy harbour. Turn right at
the tarmac, but when the road swings left, break off right
on a footpath which will lead out to the main coast road.
Turn right, passing the leading lights for the harbour (one
above, one below the A917). Opposite Lomond Terrace
(church on the corner) turn right for a path that leads
steeply down to the harbour. Subsidence destroyed this
path some years ago, but it has been rebuilt, thankfully.

Crail Harbour

Crail is the most pho-tographed or painted harbour along the East Neuk coast and the quiet state now with just a few boats going after lob-sters or partans hardly makes it seem to have been the most important at one time. (Robert the Bruce granted its charter as a Royal Burgh.) Most of the buildings round the harbour are seventeenth-century. The west arm of the harbour was built by Robert Stevenson in 1826. The painted town arms on a plaque on the larg-est building points to the old customs house. Read any notices and wander out on the far, encircling harbour arm for the view. The gasworks on the bay beside the harbour was removed in 1960. (The St Andrews eyesore only went in 2003. They had to be near harbours so coal could be landed conveniently.) Coal once was dug out of open workings at Crail, and a Queen Mary coin was once found by the miners in old work-ings. Crail never industrialised, as it lacked burns for giving water power. Grain and farm produce increased its exports when the Forth & Clyde Canal was opened.

The sandy bay beyond the harbour ends at a long seaward-running reef, then there's a short reach of sand and boulders, another reef, and beyond this is an obvi-ous angled slab at the foot of the shaly cliff. A fossil tree will be found at that spot, the stump as if sawn off above the spreading roots, while various pieces of trunk lie around.

From the harbour, head up Shoregate with its attrac-tive old houses. St Adrian's, named after the early missionary, has blue shutters and a half-figure over the door. Go up the steps (as the road bends) to follow airy Castle Walk. One looks down on St Adrian's garden and Maggie Inglis' Hole as this bit of coast is called. There's an old sundial and view indicator on the corner. The castle has long gone. The building at the end of Castle Walk was a watch house, dated 1782.

Once there turn left up a short road with garages on the left, but, first, briefly, turn down right to read the display telling about the King's Mills which once stood here. Past the garages, turn right (into Rumford) which leads on to the wide Nethergate, which with Market Street, were the well-planned extensions when the town spread out from the harbour area. (Hotels and B & Bs are to be found on the Nethergate.) Cross over to pass the row of cottages, restored by the NTS under its Little Houses scheme. The last has the lower floor corner cut in to allow traffic to pass; go through this gap and turn sharp left to walk towards the Crail Pottery (worth a visit) then turn right up Rose Wynd which leads to the High Street.

Crail Tolbooth

Turn right to come on the old tolbooth which shows a strong Dutch influence (and a Dutch bell, dated 1520, which, till recently, rang a curfew at 22.00). The weather vane is a Crail capon. The building now holds the library and local council offices. Beside it is the Crail Museum and seasonal tourist office. At the tolbooth corner with the flagpole is a *loupin on stane* (a mounting block to assist riders onto horseback).

Along wide Marketgate from the tolbooth is a granite fountain commemorating Queen Victoria's Jubilee (1897) and the reconstructed mercat cross of which only the shaft is old. The markets, dating back to Robert the Bruce's time, were held on Sundays until the Reformation. There are many fine seventeenth and eighteenth-century town houses as we walk along eastwards. One marriage lintel

Crail

is dated 1619, the earliest we've met. At the corner for the church gates at the far end of Marketgate is an erratic boulder, the Blue Stone, which tradition has it, came from the May Island. The devil had taken a scunner at Crail kirk folk and threw a big stone at the place; splitting in the air, one piece went flying on to Balcomie, while this piece came very near hitting the church.

That would have been a pity, for Crail Kirk is hoary with history. Dedicated to St Maelrubha of Applecross in

1243, it later became St Mary's and also a collegiate church. Knox preached here and James Sharp (later archbishop) was one of its ministers. Proximity to St Andrews meant frequent involvement in church and state affairs. Major alterations were made in 1796, 1815 and 1963, the tower is thirteenth-century, and inside there are quite a few features of note: early carved oak panels, a painted panel from the sailors' loft and a restored thirteenth-century lancet window with beautiful modern glass, more recent glass in the tower and a rather worn Pictish stone moved from near Fife Ness. The tower has grooves where mediaeval archers sharpened their arrow tips.

The kirkyard has a unique number of early mural monuments, some sixteenth-century. Behind the church there is a mort-house where bodies were kept locked up till decayed beyond use to body snatchers. A tablet informs, 'Erected for securing the dead'. On a cheerier note the east side of the graveyard and Denburn Wood beyond become massed with snowdrops in the spring. From the rear of the churchyard walk down Denburn Wood (Rude Well) to return to the Marketgate.

Crail's name is given variously on old maps. One I've seen had Carell and, on the same map, backtracking, would you recognise Sandness (Pittenweem), Leauins Mouth, Kirk Caldey, Pretticur, Kinghorne and Brunt Iland? The town had and has a feeling of being somewhat apart. A Glaswegian asked, last century, if he had been to America, replied 'No, but I've a brother who has been to Crail'. It is a good place to pause before the inescapable longest and hardest day of walking the Fife Coast.

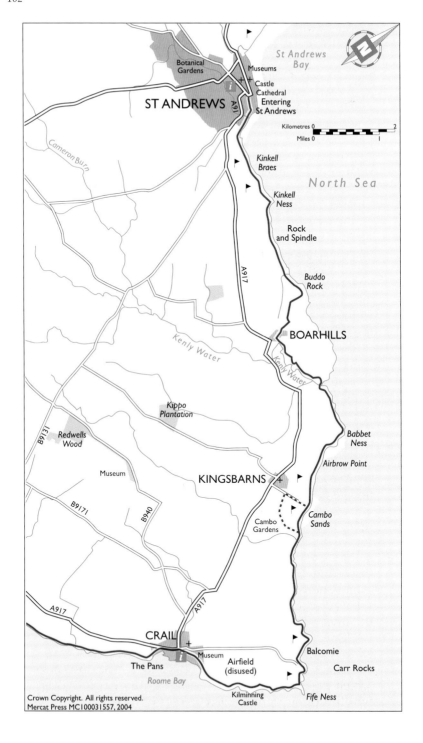

VII
Crail to St Andrews
(The Cold Coast)
O.S. 59

If you have stayed in Crail overnight perhaps you can ask for a Crail *capon* for breakfast–a haddock done local fashion. I doubt if you will be fulfilling the recommendations of an old guide (in its chapter on 'Swimming, Sailing and Drowning') which points out, 'It is one of Crail's recreative laws which, it is hoped, will be honourably observed, that Roome Bay is available for gentlemen only up till eight o'clock in the morning'.

It is essential to be away as early as possible, for today's walk can take a good eight hours and is by far the roughest and toughest day–many grades up on anything else. For much of it there is no easy escape and no refreshments or other facilities, so carry adequate supplies, especially drinks (streams, running off farmland as they do, should not be used). The harder sections come late in the day too. If in doubt there are escapes inland to the Crail-St Andrews road (A917) at Cambo, Kingsbarns and Boarhills (limited bus service) and one could plan to do this anyway if a long, hard, challenging day does not appeal. Many parts of the route are muddy or jungly, there are frequent switchbacks, a couple of places are impassible at full tide and there is a danger of landslips. It will be a long time before the official FCP is perfected: even some upgraded places have been washed out. Walkers, perforce, must be prepared to boulder hop, scramble and slither. You have been warned! Kept for a good, dry day, this 'Cold Coast' ('Golf Coast'), offers open, spacious, atmospheric, wild coastal walking quite unlike anywhere else on the coast and should be relished for those qualities.

Head off along the Nethergate or, from Marketgate take Kirk Wynd, opposite the church, which leads down to the east end of the Nethergate. From there walk the path which passes the white sixteenth-century doocot. (It is worth turning right for 50m. along the seaside path to see the doocot better, and why it is called the Pepper Pot. Unusually, there is no string course.) An erratic boulder on a reef offshore is the Mermaid's Cradle. Head off round Roome Bay, passing the children's play area. The bay ends at red cliffs which have eroded badly and forced a pedestrian diversion, so we go up steps and through by the end houses before swinging back to the coast. A last view of Crail shows how good a sea mark the doocot makes.

Walk straight through the smart Sauchope Links Caravan Park (where there's a shop). This lies on the site of a golf course that predated Balcomie, Crail's original links. The caravan site is on the lower raised beach level (about 5000 years old) while Crail largely occupies a higher raised beach some 15,000 years old. Continue on by the path which keeps close to the shore below the obvious raised beach slope. (The sea is cutting into it now too.) The lumpy rock on the point ahead is Kilminning Castle, a natural sandstone outcrop, and is at the start of the Kilminning Coast Wildlife Reserve (SWT). The bay beyond has a boulder beach and ends at a wartime machine gun post. Cattle graze this end of the reserve to reduce the rank growth and encourage a greater biodiversity. Above, mercifully not seen, is the old airfield of HMS *Jackdaw* with its decaying buildings. The Fleet Air Arm station was built on the site of the village called Goats. German bombers raided the airfield: Crail received several hits and there were fatalities in St Andrews. (Car boot sales, go-karting and other recreational efforts are altering the airfield now.) Parts of the path can become somewhat overgrown with gorse, thorn and brambles, not very user-friendly. The fenced-off areas on the second bay protect small areas of sea marsh. The path rises towards a big shed and leaves the reserve though we are still in an SSSI (Site of Special Scientific Interest). Suddenly the mast and coastguard buildings on the Ness lie just ahead.

The 1998 creation of the Craighead Links (golf course) lies to the left, behind a good example of new dry-stane dyking. We drop down and along to 'the end of Fife', Foreland Head or **Fife Ness**, passing under the more imposing buildings of the coastguard station then wend up to squeeze by the thrust of grey rock below the unspectacular light. There's a Fife Bird Club hide and

Fife Ness

another old machine gun post built by Polish forces in 1941. Turn right, between them, for the last view back to the Forth estuary and the now distant marks of May Island, Bass Rock and North Berwick Law. The grey rocks below are strangely worn, and a contrast to the jagged basalt strata running out just round the corner when we pass under the light. The Forth has expanded from the river we crossed into Fife; the distance from here over to Dunbar is something over 30km. (19 miles).

For most walkers the main interest will be the stiff-winged fulmars which skim the cliff thermals all along the coast. They arrive early in the year and leave at summer's end, staying out at sea over the winter. They only start breeding when seven years old and only lay a single egg, yet the twentieth century saw their breeding range expand from a few remote islands off NW Scotland to encircle the British Isles. Gannets, blazing white with black wing tips, the Concorde of the seas, are also likely to be seen, the Bass Rock being one of the world's biggest breeding sites. The Bass is such an historic site that the bird is actually named after it: *Sula bassana*. Watching gannets diving can seriously delay walkers! Eiders bob and croon among the rocks. The Forth Estuary has over 20% of the UK's population of these crooners.

The Carr Rocks and Fife Ness generally have seen a score of ships lost (listed in B. Baird's *Shipwrecks of the Forth*), three being paddle steamers: *Windsor Castle* 1844,

At Fife Ness

Queen 1857 and *Commodore* 1859. Another paddle steamer took the name *Commodore* and was also wrecked, at St Andrews, in 1896.

The small tarred road is joined and curves round past several caravans facing what was once Fife Ness harbour. This was mostly natural and occupied an exposed and dangerous site–yet it was here Mary of Guise landed before going on to St Andrews to marry James V. At one time stone was exported to Rotterdam. If you look carefully on the north shore you may see the circle of an inter-tidal spring, then a more obvious larger stone circle in the rocks, which gives rise to all manner of speculative ideas, but the true explanation is that it is an archaeological site to do with the notorious Carr Rocks. Further out lies the Bell Rock which, in 1799 alone, sank 70 ships, and when Robert Stevenson, having managed to erect a light there (a saga worth pursuing), he was asked to tackle the Carr Rocks, the reef off Fife Ness.

The old harbour was restored for landing the stone, which was cut with this circle as the template for the dove-tailed stones. A tower was planned and a coffer dam had to be created on every visit to the reefs, so in 1813, the first year, only 41 hours of labour was possible, in 1814 only 53 and in 1815 most of the work was destroyed by the sea. It took two more years to complete only to be utterly destroyed again. They gave up. A cage-like marker on iron legs was built on the base in steel, easy enough to replace when need be. Now a single pole carries a radar reflector. There's an explanation board at the site. Older folk can recall a red lightship which now sits in Dundee harbour.

Keep round the sea's edge to another display board at the site of a one-time tidal mill. Return, briefly, to the road. The oddity of a village pump stands by the road, the only indication of a hamlet at Fife Ness long ago. Turn off to pass between golf course and the tidal pool. White markers indicate the edge of the Crail Golfing Society's course and walkers are asked not to stroll on the golf course.

The Crail Golfing Society was founded in 1786 and is the seventh oldest golf club in the world. The markers show the crest of the Crail 'ship' topped by eighteenth-century golf sticks. The attractive course was first laid out by Old Tom Morris.

Round a first point, on the left of the track, stands a cave. Tradition has it as Constantine's Cave, where the king was killed, *c.*874, at the hands of raiding Danes. Sandy Balcomie Bay now sweeps ahead. The obvious building on the dunes has roundels above the walled-up seaward side showing its earlier use as a lifeboat station: a crown over 1884 on one, the other a lifeboat above the letters RNLBI. At the end of the sand is the Blue Stone, the other erratic paired in legend with the one at the gates of Crail church. Inland we can just glimpse Balcomie Castle where Mary of Guise had B&B in 1538. Now it is part of a farm.

There are two golf courses now at Balcomie, so they extend well round the bay with white markers throughout. Keep to the banks by the shore beyond to swing round to a stile below the headland. Do

Balcomie

not go up/inland. Cliffs (fulmars overhead) fall sheer to the sea with no real alternative (except waiting) if the tide is right up. A secondary prow also entails a tidal passage before one can gain the edge of cultivation–and yet another golf course, the highly-praised Kingsbarns links.

One can walk on shore or along the edge of fields/ golf course to reach the bridges over the **Cambo Burn**. The larger bridge with the decorative letter K has been made to blend with the 'Japanese' footbridge seen up-stream. Seaward is a footbridge for golfers who play along the sea's margin to the exposed 15th hole out on the point.

The Cambo Burn comes down through attractive woodlands and it is worth a diversion, both for itself and to visit the walled garden. Walk up beside the burn (masses of snowdrops, daffodils and hyacinths in sea-son) past the graceful curved footbridge and then cross at a second. Ground and trees at one spot are swamped in ivy. The path heads on to pass left of the walled gar-den and out to the main road, but turn right before the walled garden to follow its wall (by a pool) along to the entrance. (Open: 10.00-dusk; honesty box payment.) There is interest at any time of the year. If you walk out onto the parkland beyond you can see Cambo House (flats) and, across the park, a fancy architectural doocot (a tower with finials), the sort of thing that followed the beehive and lectern types we've seen so often. The Cambo

Cambo Gardens

name comes from a grant by William the Lion to the de
Cambhou family. An Erskine bought the estate in 1668
and it has remained in their family ever since. The lush
setting is quite a surprise on the Cold Coast. Return to
the sea by keeping to the path down the right/south bank.
The FCP has an alternative here of going up the glen a bit
from the K bridge and then heading inland round the
golf course, but most walkers I'm sure will want to keep
to the coast.

From the bridge over the Cambo Burn follow the track
on to circle the trees right (where there is a 'Restrooms'
building) then break off on a path at the seaward 15th
green. Follow the dunes along the edge of this undulating new golf course, crossing one burn, to come out at a
car park/picnic area (with seasonal toilets), served by a
road down from Kingsbarns. At most tides it is possible
to walk along the warm-coloured sands. The road leads
up to the A917 at Kingsbarns, an old hamlet where the
king did once collect and store grain for use at Crail or
Falkland. Remains of a harbour can be seen once past
the toilet block. We continue walking along the edge of
the golf course, the last green edged with an enormous
bunker. At a wall running down to the sea there's a warning that the going ahead can be 'hazardous/tidal' but
this should only seriously affect passage on rare occasions. Nearing Airbow Point the thin path line drops
down to the sand and on by a green chalet on the point.

The view ahead looks stark and bare with parallel reefs
running out to sea. After Babbet Ness we are walking
nearly *west* and it is the Angus coast we see off-right. A
jagged, hard sandstone overlies a softer one, sand laid
down in moving water rather than lake bed, so we are
seeing, so to speak, a petrified torrent. Partridges are common on this coast; you may well have been startled by
them taking off at your feet. We come on areas with wall-
ing built up against the sea's erosion, the first bit of wall
(at the end of a small bay) being on bands of coal and
shale. On top of the rocks are the *stigmaria* (imprints) of
prehistoric roots (of *Lepidodendron* or *Sigillaria*). From the
red pantiled ruin (an old salmon bothy) we follow a farm
track; keep to the branch along outside the walled field–
to reach the barrier of the Kenly Water. Kenly is from the
Gaelic *cean liath*, grey head.

The Kenly Water can be paddled at low tide (never boulder hop!) but the going beyond is neither interesting nor easy enough to make this worthwhile, so the best route (and the FCP) turns inland for a pleasant enough diversion. In winter and spring the woods are massed with snowdrops, anemones, primroses and wild hyacinths in turn. You may spot a dipper, and wrens are noisily present.

Just before reaching the cottages of Hillhead the FCP drops down, right, to wend alongside the Kenly Water, a woody dell that seems quite surprising on this wild coast. A side stream comes in at a ruined mill, dated 1716 on a gable. Across the stream there are cottages with colourful gardens. We pass several gooseberry bushes and there are various ruins on our bank while, across the Kenly, sprawl the barns of Burnside Farm. Cross the footbridge and walk up by the attractive farmhouse.

Turn left and follow the road up a brae which brings Boarhills into view. When the road swings left take the dirt track off right to follow field edges along to massive green barns. Turn right round the barns (note the red-tiled *doocot*) and then break off, first right, on a green track which leads back to the shore. A gate/stile gives access to the curve of bay with the strange feature of the **Buddo Rock** prominent. On clear days the Angus hills can be seen and towns as far up the coast as Arbroath.

The main bulk of the Buddo Rock, a pink sandstone, has a cap across to a beaked pillar and, unexpectedly, there

Buddo Rock

High seas off Kenly

is a split up the rock so it can be climbed–adventurously
–with the help of some steps and holds carved out.

At the time of writing the official FCP onwards has
several problems and some damaging landslips. The following may be outdated by alterations which can only
be improvements. The warnings on p.xi should be un-
derstood clearly.

There are some shallow caves in the cliff beyond Buddo
Rock. Follow the path over the wall to angle up to the
top of the bank. The first of many landslips will be seen
here. (One can also avoid this headland by keeping along
beside the shore.) The St Andrews Bay golf course/com-
plex sprawls inland. There's a boundary stone (H on top)
looking like a trig point on the prow of Buddo Ness. We
drop down again to traverse the wildest single section of
the day's walk, a west-coast sort of switchback of narrow path through scrub and rock, with plenty bracken
and blackthorn and scented with honeysuckle in season.
At another dell the path returns to the shore.

Kittock's Den only has a small stream, so presents no
problem (*kittock* is a giddy lassie!). The prow beyond is
the site of a prehistoric fort. Kittock's Den comes down
from Boarhills and the jungly scrub is a haven for winter
migrants blown in off the North Sea. I've seen redwing
and fieldfare passing like blowing leaves in November.
The very lucky might see waxwing in winter after an
eastern gale.

The path twists up to run along above the wall (except at high tide the shore can as easily be followed) to round a prow where landslip is held by wattle fencing. The bay ahead has a jagged pinnacle, but before it is reached the path climbs (by steps) brutally up to regain the golf course edge again. A dell is substantially bridged, then the path drops down, right, through a thorn 'tunnel', eventually to regain the shoreline. Ahead is the striking feature of the **Rock and Spindle**.

The Rock and Spindle

Either walk the shore or bits of path above if the tide so dictates. There's one awkward corner just before a crag forces the walker to be-low high tide level for a unique stile (actually built below high water mark!). The path along the green slopes is unfor-tunately shared with cattle, and, at low tide, the shore is pleasanter till past the Rock and Spindle. At high tide the path climbs up (facing the Rock and Spindle) to a spur, dips, joins a farm track, *descends* and works round by stepping stones/path (not seen from above) to gain a longer easy stretch of coast.

The base of the Rock and Spindle has a circle of basalt rays ('like the rays of a daisy') and little imagination is needed to envisage a bubble of lava exploding to create it. The whole is a volcanic plug; all that is left of a weath-ered eruption of lava that burst through the sandstone millennia ago. The slender pinnacle can be climbed, an easy but exposed task, but that is a game best left to the climbers. The cart tracks coming down to the coast here led to a now vanished harbour, and local farmers also took up seaweed to manure their fields.

Following the easy section the path climbs (more steps) very steeply up for bold Kinkell Ness. From the Ness St

Maiden Rock

Andrews (at last?) appears clearer and nearer. This area is called the Kinkell Braes. Nearing the caravan park, take a descending path (some steps again) to pass along above the Maiden Rock, another isolated sandstone feature which has been a rock-climbing school for many novices. The first mention is by the great Harold Raeburn, who wrote, in 1902, that he found 'the complete traverse of the arête a nice little climb'. A path leads down to the shore, but it is really easier just to keep along the braes. (The rocks beyond the Maiden are full of *encrinites*: the fossil remains of cylinder-shaped sea creatures which show clearly as white circles in the darker matrix. Kinkell is *ceann coille*, head of the wood. The path goes along by the caravan site* where there is older subsidence showing, to descend to the East Sands, the bay curving round to the harbour with its long sheltering arm. The cathedral ruins dominate the view. The tarred footway runs along past the East Sands Leisure Centre, the Gatty Marine Laboratory (St Andrews University had the first ever marine laboratory), Sailing Club (in the old lifeboat building; there's a good snackbar) and putting green. In 1864 a severe storm washed up a sea worm 55 metres (180ft.

* Winter 2003 saw a major landslip here: a fifty yard stretch reaching back into the caravan park collapsed (leaving the fences of the coastal path suspended across the gap like a Himalayan footbridge)–a serious break, which may or may not be dealt with by the time this is read.

long) on the East Sands. A footbridge crosses the gates of
the inner harbour which now only sees a few pleasure
craft, rather than a one time fishing fleet which operated
in these dangerous waters. It has a sluice to let water out
to clear sand from the outer harbour.

Turn right along by the flats, whose level roofs make
them the most inept restoration seen on our walk. The
harbour arm is long and, as most do, gives a worthwhile
view from its far end. On Sunday morning students still
walk the pier wearing traditional red gowns. The harbour arm was built in the winter of 1655 by women from
the Netherlands. From the back of the flats walk up under the old signal station to the site of the Church of St
Mary on the Rock, a twelfth-century foundation (see the
descriptive notice board). Little is visible, and the site was
only discovered when constructing a coastal battery in
1860. Two cannons face out to sea and there's a view along
the cliffs to the castle. The cliff top walk is a delight, and
you'll be eye-to-eye probably with the nesting fulmars,
'planing the thermals with insolent skill'. The first fulmars (once a rare northern bird) first nested here in 1947
in their gradual colonisation right round the British coast.

The path forks: the right fork leads along the cliffs, past
the Castle, along the Scores to Murray Park (left, far end)
which has many accommodation options, the left fork
comes out to the end of North Street and on round outside

Approaching St Andrews

St Andrews Castle from St Rule's Tower

the cathedral becomes South Street. Market Street lies between. North Street is largely taken up with university
buildings, South Street and Market Street are more commercial. Other B & Bs tend to be on the outskirts; there
are several hundred options–unless there's a major golf
tournament in progress! The Tourist Office is in the middle of Market Street (no. 70), and it would be worth a
visit now to pick up a town map and anything else of
local interest. Accommodation can be booked there too.

116

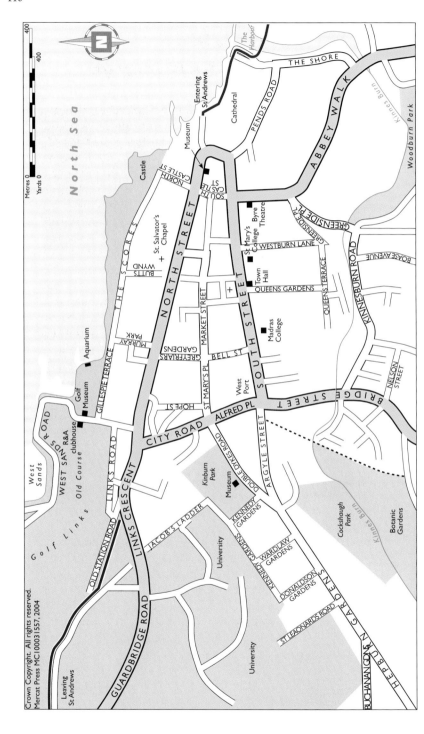

VIII
Exploring St Andrews

This exploration of St Andrews is described as a single walkabout, but you would need to be strong-legged and have ' 'satiable curiosity' to fit in everything mentioned, so either be selective or spread the walking over two or three days. If a visit was not made previously, do call on the centrally-sited Tourist Office (70 Market Street) to obtain a town map and the current information on *What's On*.

St Andrews originally had the name Kilrymont, but with the legendary arrival of the apostle's relics it became St Andrews. The relics were supposedly brought by St Rule (St Regulus), but he was a Celtic missionary with no local connection. A Northumbrian connection may be more likely, as Hexham was known to have housed relics of the saint and these may have been bought or brought on to St Andrews. David I granted the town's charter *c*.1144. Like many old towns it was once walled; unlike most, one of the ports (entrances) has survived, and we'll start our perambulation at this, the **West Port**.

The gateway was reconstructed in 1589. In 1650 Charles II was presented with the key of the city here. Now it demands a one-way traffic system. Head off along South Street. The Gifford tome has comments on almost every house; we'll, perforce, be more selective. On the right there is an older house with a forestair and the oval logo of the St Andrews Preservation Trust, which was founded in 1937 to rescue and restore some of the classic domestic architecture. St Andrews too was lucky that a retired military type from India became provost in the 1840s, and went about rebuilding the civic spirit and its historic buildings and monuments. There's a mural monument to Sir Hugh Playfair in the cathedral cemetery and a Playfair Aisle in the historic Town Kirk. The minister then was another Playfair; his monument is an elaborate marble pulpit. The initials of previous ministers who had been Moderators of the Church of Scotland decorated this pulpit, including Playfair's, but no room was left for subsequent initials and, strangely, the kirk has not produced a Moderator since!

St Andrews Cathedral

On the right, look down Louden's Close, typical of the old runrig system. Walking on, still on the right one comes on a small ruin, which is all that remains of the Blackfriars Monastery with the imposing Madras College behind, across the lawns. The ruin is the apse of the 1525 chapel. The monastery was smashed following John Knox's 1559 St Andrews sermon. (Knox had earlier been imprisoned in the castle and spent some time as a galley slave in France.) As in most places in the town there are interpretative display boards. The 'suave Jacobean manor' was built by William Burn and opened in 1834, founded by Dr Andrew Bell, a local lad, son of a hairdresser, who worked in the USA, was ordained and went as a missionary to India where he worked out his Madras monitorial system. The school was co-educational, unusual for the time. The fine façade hid somewhat Spartan realities; one rector wrote of donning two sets of woollen underwear in October and keeping them on till April. Some classes started at 06.00.

Cross the street to go through a pend (passage) to cobbled Burgher Close, a typical courtyard. When you come out, turn left past the post office where a plaque commemorates John Adamson, pioneer photographer, who took the first ever calotype photo in 1841. We then come on the **Town Kirk**, Holy Trinity, the roof covered in Caithness slabs, the chancel floor Iona marble and with a blaze of stained glass. Only the tower is old (*c*.1410). Entering, the many-pillared arches recall the great mosque at Cordoba. Gifford calls the church 'a dictionary of architectural quotations'. The tower was often used for locking up sinful women, and cutty stools (repentance seats) and the branks point to intolerant times.

The branks were an iron head-fitting frame with a bar into the mouth to make speech impossible. Archbishop Sharp had the branks on one Isobel Lindsay to stop her heckling during his sermons. He was to be murdered on Magus Moor above St Andrews not long after. Hackston of Rathillet, one of the ringleaders of the assassination, was judicially butchered and parts of his body hung up in various towns as a warning. A huge near-contemporary marble monument shows the hated archbishop's end. In 1849 when his tomb was opened it only contained a broken coffin and no sign of human remains. This was where John Knox preached his rabble-rousing sermon in 1559 which led to the direct destruction of much church property. Old Tom Morris, the Royal and Ancient's first professional golfer, has a memorial, among many others.

Diagonally across from the church is the baronial pile of the 1858 town hall, which replaced the Market Street tolbooth. There are associated mementos on display. Provosts are listed back to the twelfth century. Royal Burghs only lost their unique character in 1975 government reorganisation. The clock hangs over the street, a Polish memorial and provost lamps on the side street.

Beyond the church is the Tudor-style building where the *St Andrews Citizen* has been published since 1870. The site was the home of Bailie Bell, the father of Madras College's founder, who had a mechanical flair and worked with an Alexander Wilson on a system of type founding that made their names. Wilson was associated with a Philadelphia foundry and cast the first-ever $ sign (in 1797).

Turn left along Church Street, which was originally Kirk Wynd before gentrification, to reach Market Street, the old heart of the town where cobbled crosses indicate the past sites of mercat cross and tolbooth. There is a Saturday street market, and the Lammas Fair in early August is the oldest surviving mediaeval fair in Scotland, dating back to 1153 at least. Five fairs once attracted pilgrims and traders from all over Europe. Latterly the Lammas

Fair was largely a fee-ing fair (for signing on farm workers) and now is simply a funfair. The fountain is a
memorial to novelist George Whyte-Melville who died
in a hunting accident. The hapless Chastelard (caught in
Mary Queen of Scotland's bedroom–twice) was executed
here in 1563 and so was the Bohemian reformer, Paul
Craw, who was slowly burned to death in 1433, a brass
ball forced into his mouth to prevent him speaking to the
crowd.

Cross Market Street onto College Street to reach North
Street. **St Salvator's Church** tower dominates the scene.
Between North Street and the sea the area is largely university buildings. Bishop Wardlaw was the recognised
founder of higher studies in St Andrews in 1410, based
on Orleans. A papal bull two years later confirmed what
was to be Scotland's first university (in Britain only Oxford and Cambridge are older). St Salvator's College was
founded by Bishop Kennedy in 1450. The Kate Kennedy
Procession each April recalls some of this history, Kate's
part being played by a 'beardless *bejant*', as first year male
students are called.

The tower at first had no steeple, and in 1546 the Protestants who had seized the castle were bombarded by
French cannon from the top of the tower. In front of the
pend through the foot of the tower the initials PH on the
cobbles indicates where Patrick Hamilton, a young, well-
connected and likeable student, was burned in 1528–the
deed taking several hours. Walk through the pend to the
Jacobean-style quadrangle and the entrance to the church
is on the right, the interior gloriously rich and colourful.
Bishop Kennedy's tomb and John Knox's pulpit are preserved and there are monuments to old boy Andrew
Lang, the Borders poet, historian and folklorist. One keen
golfer who studied at St Andrews was the Marquis of
Montrose. Among the Rectors of the University have been
Andrew Carnegie and James Barrie–and the Norwegian
explorer Nansen. More recently they've had John Cleese
and Frank Muir.

Return to Market Street and, near the Tourist Office,
go through Crails Lane to South Street, then cross over to
the archway entrance to **St Mary's College's** attractive
quadrangle. The holm oak dates to 1728, but centuries
earlier is the propped-up thorn by the bell tower, planted,

tradition claims, by the ubiquitous Mary Queen of Scots. Archbishop Beaton founded the college in 1539. The buildings on the east side include the James VI library, gifted in 1612. In 1645 the Scottish Estates met here, and the room has been Parliament Hall ever since. The sundial dates to 1664. The French influence is due to French workers being borrowed from the construction of the palace at Falkland.

Knox preaching at St Andrews
(display in the Castle)

Continue eastwards along South Street, lined with sturdy old town houses of character. Janetta's is a justly famous ice cream parlour: over 30 flavours to choose from. South Court Pend leads to a courtyard, lit in season by a flowering cherry tree. A plaque commemorates Professor J D Forbes, one of the early alpinists and the scientist who astonished contemporaries by showing that glaciers were 'rivers of ice'. Abbey Street, next along, right, has the Byre Theatre where the original tiny (73 seats) theatre was created in a byre (cowshed) in 1933. It has been rebuilt twice since. Continuing along South Street, the cathedral ruins are framed at the end of the street with, left, the leaning corner tower of the Roundel and, right, Queen Mary's House. The gateway beyond is the Pends (an old priory entrance) and leads to the harbour. As you swing left, another cobbled cross before the Deans Court gateway marks where the 80-year-old Walter Myln, apprehended at Dysart, burned at the stake in 1558 on the orders of Archbishop Hamilton, himself to be executed in 1571 for being involved in the murder of Darnley. Henry Forrest, another student, also suffered here in 1533. Cross the road to enter the **Cathedral** grounds.

The building itself is a 'rent skeleton' (Ruskin) but, at

over 100m. long, it still indicates past glory. Display
boards describe the scene. The museum in the old refur-
bished priory buildings should not be missed, the early
sarcophagus panels being one of Scotland's most treasured and breathtakingly beautiful antiquities. There are
many assembled gravestones; one, on a windowsill,
shows death as a skeleton stabbing his victim in the back.
In the entrance is a slab with several 'Green Men' worked
into the patterning. A token purchased in the museum
will give access to the 33m. high, square, St Rule's Tower,
the finest viewpoint in St Andrews. Within the east side
choir there's a mural slab showing a skeleton lying in a
hammock. Facing it is a monument to Dr Thomas
Chalmers, who was Professor of Divinity among all his
other activities. A walk round the wall of the graveyard
will produce everything from full-rigged ships to golfers
like Tom Morris, father and son, and Willie Auchterlonie,
the last local to win the Open–in 1893. Tom Morris, sen-
ior, won the second-ever Open in 1861 and then again in
1862, 1864 and 1867. His 17-year-old son won it in 1868,
1869, 1870 (no championship in 1871) and 1872, the first
ever four-in-a-row. Young Tom died aged 24. James
Anderson, of a golf-ball-making local family, won three
in a row, 1877—1879. Golf has to be added to Town and
Gown as the St Andrews triumvirate.

The Cathedral had an unhappy history. The west front
was wrecked in a storm, Edward I of England stripped

Early golf-ball maker (St Andrews Golf Museum)

the lead off the roof, and fifty years later it was gutted by fire and took seven years to restore. One bishop, captured by English pirates, refused to be ransomed in order not to sidetrack funds. At the time of Bishop Wardlaw the south transept was blown down. In 1472 it became the metropolitan see, and for a century nothing fell down or went up in flames. In 1559, however, the Reformation instigated the 'burning of images and mass-books and breaking of altars', and the Cathedral became a quarry for building stone for the town. The Cathedral was originally consecrated by Bishop Lamberton, staunch ally of Robert the Bruce (who was present), and for crowning Bruce at Scone, Edward I had the bishop put in chains.

From the Cathedral head along North Street. Left is the St Andrews Preservation Trust Museum, with displays of grocer's and chemist's shops from more recent, more peaceful, times. Not for long though; turn right into North Castle Street (ex-Castle Wynd) and head for the **Castle** visible ahead. Cobbled initials this time point to where George Wishart was burned in 1546 while Cardinal Beaton looked on from a castle window. Not long after a small gang of Protestants managed to seize the Castle–and the cardinal's body was hung out of the same window. Henry VIII backed the Protestants, who held out for a year. The Castle was 'dang doon' several times before that, though. Little of the structure survives (the harbour was repaired by pillaging its stone) but the Visitor Centre has a fascinating audio-visual display telling the story of the fortress. Two features are notable however: in the Sea Tower is the Bottle Dungeon, and one can explore a mine and counter mine. The former is carved out of solid rock, bottle-shaped, the only access via a rope lowered down the 'neck'. No one ever escaped its dark, dank depths, and the sea was there for taking the victims' bodies. (The sea has now taken the whole east range with its Great Hall.) In a 1546 siege the Earl of Arran began to mine towards the castle walls to lay explosive charges, quite an undertaking as the passage was big enough for ponies to pack off the rock. The tunnel sloped to pass under the defensive ditch, and a chamber was prepared under the walls, only for a desperately-searching counter mine to break through and spoil the attempt. Going through these tunnels is a memorable experience.

St Andrews Botanical Gardens

The street leading along westwards from the castle is The Scores (ex Swallowgait), at the far end of which are several other features, but they, I'm sure, would need another day after this marathon walkabout. They deserve a mention however. Fulmars nest on the cliffs and the Aquarium lies below, its largest 'pool' the old Step Rock tidal swimming pool, much used in hardier times. Witch Hill with the Martyrs' Monument and trim bandstand is also the old Bow Butts, where archery was practised. In 1457 James II tried to ban golf (and football) as archery was being neglected. Both James VI and his mother were great at the 'gowf'. The British Golf Museum is bunkered into the hill, a high-tech, fascinating place with old mementos and audio-visual displays. You can see historic replays, brush up on history, follow the careers of the greats and lots more. The Royal and Ancient Golf Club is just across the road and the historic Old Course (and others) lead away along the West Sands to the Eden estuary. The ladies' putting green is nicknamed The Himalayas. The West Sands give several kilometres of walking, usually with a snell wind. The setting was used for the opening sequence in the film *Chariots of Fire*. Do walk along the sands, perhaps to round off the day. Out Head, the far end, is a nature reserve, and from the high point there's a view to the dunes stretching away by Tentsmuir to the Tay Estuary.

In 1991 the St Andrews Museum opened in a castellated mansion in Kinburn Park, telling the story of the town with modern aids (you can see, hear and even smell it!). In the gardens is the Sikorski memorial, commemorating the wartime leader of the Polish forces. The museum is on Doubledykes Road, the continuation westwards of Market Street, and nearby, too, is the 18-acre site of the impressive Botanical Gardens, a 10-minute walk from the West Port. The Kinness Burn site is attractive at all times, and there are large glasshouse collections, demonstrations etc. The Cacti House has over 250 species, there's an orchid house and collections of alpines, rhododendrons, primulas and aquatic plants, all in a magnificent tree-rich setting.

The Kinness Burn, which flows through the heart of the city into the harbour, gives a delightfully rural walk and is recommended. Several of the *wynds* south from South Street lead to a path, which can also be joined from Argyll Street (East Port, continuation westwards), which leads along the Lade Braes Walk.

In mediaeval times pilgrims from all over England and the continent *walked* all the way to St Andrews. This rather puts our brief expedition into perspective, but we become, having shared the physical and mental stimulus of exploring the Fife coast and St Andrews, part of the long tradition.

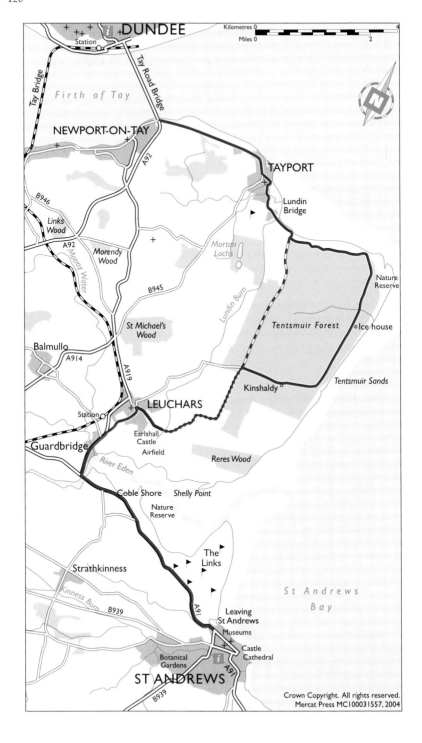

DUNDEE

Station

Tay Bridge

Tay Road Bridge

Kilometres 0   4
Miles 0   2

Firth of Tay

NEWPORT-ON-TAY

TAYPORT

A92

B946

Lundin
Bridge

Links
Wood

A92

Morendy
Wood

Moray Water

Morton
Lochs

B945

Nature
Reserve

Lundin Burn

St Michael's
Wood

Tentsmuir Forest

Ice house

Balmullo

A914

A919

Tentsmuir Sands

Kinshaldy

LEUCHARS

Station

Earlshall
Castle
Airfield

Guardbridge

River Eden

Reres Wood

Coble Shore

Shelly Point

Nature
Reserve

The
Links

St Andrews

Bay

Strathkinness

Kinness Burn

B939

A91

Leaving
St Andrews

Museums

Castle
Cathedral

Botanical
Gardens

ST ANDREWS

A91

B939

IX
By Tentsmuir to the Tay Bridge
O.S. 59

The only easy option for the FCP from St Andrews to Guard Bridge, the lowest bridging point on the River Eden, was to follow the Millennium Cycle Way which runs close–all too close–beside the busy A91. Possible alternatives along the coast or using the course of the railway (which may be erroneously shown as cycle way on the Landranger map) are not really practical even if time allowed.

Head out westwards from the roundabout on North Street. As the main road swings left take the dead-end road, right, Gibson Place, with the Old Course Hotel very obvious ahead. The historic Old Course lies to the right, with the picturesque Swilcan Bridge leading up to the Eighteenth Hole and the R & A Club House–a scene well known from Open Championship coverage on TV. The Open comes to St Andrews periodically. Winners, working backwards over the last few, have been Tiger Woods (2000), John Daly (1995), Nick Faldo (1990), Seve Ballesteros (1984), Jack Nicklaus (1978 and 1970), Tony Lema (1964), Kel Nagle (1960–the Centenary Open) and Bobby Locke (1957).

The Millennium Open at St Andrews

The Society of St Andrews Golfers was formed in 1754 and became the game's regulatory body. The 'Royal' was added to the title when William IV became patron. The clubhouse was built in 1854. There are several courses on these links: the Old Course (so old it can't be dated), the New Course (1895), the Jubilee Course (Queen Victoria's, 1897), the Eden Course (1914), the Strathyrum (1993, pronounced Strath-tye-rum) and the Balgrove beginners' course (9-holes, 1972).

Pick up the Cycle Way/FCP, left, after a small car park. There are playing fields to the left and then there's an entrance for the Eden, Strathyrum and Balgrove courses, a driving range etc. Golf is now very big business in St Andrews.

Just before the main road, turn off right on the Cycle Way/FCP path which will be our route through to Guard Bridge. There's a warning notice about golfers–who lose a penalty shot at least, I trust, for hitting walkers or cyclists. As far as the courses continue alongside there are trees between us and the A91–no doubt to protect the motorist from flying golf balls. The route is tarmac and this 3.5 miles must be the least walker-friendly part of the FCP. We lose the trees after the golf courses and then have an aromatic stretch of pig farm before the route simply becomes A91 pavement and the senses are given maximum punishment from the speeding traffic. At this juncture there is a footpath down to the local nature reserve at the Coble Shore point. On the far side is Coble House Point, and Sand Ford Head between suggests this waist in the estuary might once have been a ford.

Continuing along the A91 the paper mill at **Guard Bridge** dominates, with the big quarry behind halving hapless Lucklaw Hill. We soon come on an old toll house, recognised, as most are, by windows giving clear views both ways, in order not to miss any traffic. There's also one of east Fife's attractive cast iron milestones (St Andrews 3). Shortly, on the other side of the road, at the Strathkinnes junction, is the Hungry Horse café. On a bit, turn off right, taking an old piece of road signposted for the Guard Bridge Hotel. There are picnic tables and a good view of the inner estuary. There are also outside tables at the Guard Bridge Hotel, the walls of which are

Guard Bridge Hotel

covered in butterflies. If imbibing, do go inside to see the collection of old prints and paintings of the area. A notice on one wall caught my fancy: 'Be warned that tickling and groping is an offence under section 27 of the Salmon and Freshwater Fisheries Act 1927'.

The Eden Estuary has now narrowed to a wide tidal river, 22 miles from its source in the Lomond Hills and its course through the rich farmland heart of Fife. This lowest bridging point has been well used over the centuries. No doubt, at times, it was well guarded. We walk across one of the most historic bridges in Scotland, for it dates back to 1419. Upstream, the main road goes over a triple-arched concrete bridge, typical of its 1938 period, while downstream are the stumpy piers of the 1852 Fife Coast Railway (North British), which followed round from Leuchars Junction to St Andrews, Crail and the other East Neuk towns to Leven and Thornton Junction. The line was axed by Beeching in 1967. What a tourist lure it could have become with steam trains running on it now. The old bridge was built by Bishop Wardlaw early in the fifteenth century, which makes it one of the oldest bridges in Scotland as well as one of the most pleasing. In 1685 repairs were made from the revenues of vacant stipends and the bridge was referred to as Gair Bridge. Guard is just a corruption of this. There are bold cutwaters and six arches, the most easterly being smaller, and three refuges (recesses for pedestrians) on each parapet, which may be

of later date. Panels bear the arms and initials of Archbishop James Beaton.

Once over the River Eden turn right (on the A919 now)
into the village of Guard Bridge. There's a few surprising
buildings in brick, including a one-time church (over left),
then the impressive old facade of the 1899 Guard Bridge
Cooperative Society–note the date on a fancy gully box
and the clasped hands motif. We pass the local post of-
fice/shop, then come on the entrance to the Guardbridge
paper mill (Curtis Fine Papers Ltd) where there's the Eden
Estuary Centre.

This is simply an attractive birdwatching hide (with
disabled access, toilet) looking over the upper estuary,
and should not be missed. The whole Eden Estuary is a
local Nature Reserve and SSSI of international importance for its birdlife, the relatively pollution-free waters
ensuring plenty of mussels, cockles, snails, worms and
algae to feed the thousands of wildfowl and waders.
Shelduck and red-breasted mergansers are common, and
you could see long-tailed duck, eider, scaup, common
and velvet scoter, oyster-catcher, ringed and grey plover,
bar-tailed godwit, black-tailed godwit, redshank, curlew,
ringed plover, knot and sanderling according to season,
as well as peregrine, stonechat and garden birds. Four
species of geese over-winter. There's a useful leaflet available at the centre and recent interests are marked on a
blackboard.

Guard Bridge

Near the path to the hide the pediment of the now gone 1920 Memorial Institute marks the World War One list of those killed–33 from this hamlet. Back on the road, walk along past the trim, environmentally-conscious paper mill, with a large clock over the road. The site was origi-nally that of the Seggie Distillery (belonging to the Haig family, 1810) and there was also a pulp-mill and brick-works. When these failed, the Guardbridge Paper Company was established in the distillery building in 1873, so there has been well over a century of papermaking at Guardbridge–a famous name for this reason. Making paper I find fascinating, and these days quite a lot of waste products can be used and there's also recycling. Employ-ing 300 people, this is a large concern by today's standards, and vital locally.

We then pass over another old bridge lying on the in-land side of the A919. This was the Inner Bridge or Motray Bridge, only replaced by the new road in 1938. The Motray Water was essential for the paper-mill which, in 1967 for instance, used 20 million gallons a week (more than the town of St Andrews!). The estuary was necessary for ex-porting whisky, bone meal, wool, paper and agricultural produce, and the three piers could cope with 32 vessels which seems incredible now. Something like 200 vessels came to grief on this part of the coast, so the coming of the railway was welcomed. The paper-mill was bombed on a sneak low-level raid during World War Two, but no damage was done.

Continue on by a play area and houses to reach the Balmullo junction with the A919. Continue along the A919 briefly, turning off right, for the minor road into **Leuchars**. The road crosses the end of the runway and then through a mix of the RAF station (right) and hous-ing (left) so there's an odd feeling as women push prams along past high-security fences and guardrooms. The third weekend in September (Battle of Britain Day) sees an annual airshow which is very popular. If there is any-thing special on you will see the equivalent of twitchers along the roadside as you walk past. A 'retired' Phantom is sited just inside the main gate. A Spitfire used to be there but they are so rare and valuable now that this one was moved to a museum.

A bend suddenly brings Leuchars Church, up on its

Leuchars Church—a Romanesque treasure

knoll, into view, a startling change, for the village retains
a douce, almost mediaeval atmosphere. We turn right and
right again onto Earlshall Road, but first have a good look
at the church–and perambulate the site if the gates are
chained up. There is no drinking water between here and
Tayport, so stock up if need be.

Leuchars and Dalmeny (above Queensferry) are the
two finest Romanesque churches in Scotland, with magnificent arcading giving the prize to Leuchars. The chancel
and apse are twelfth-century, and the apse roof was replaced by the octagonal bell tower in the sixteenth century,
with a lead weathercock. Corbel heads above the upper
arches are of animals, real or imagined, and human and
grotesque faces. A papal bull mentions the church in 1187
but it was (re)-dedicated in 1244 with the name of St
Athernase. One minister, a noted preacher, Alexander
Henderson, was Moderator of the 1638 Assembly in Glasgow which abolished episcopacy.

Earlshall Road passes the primary school (on the left),
continues over a crossroads and on to Earlshall Castle,
now foreign-owned and no longer open, which is a pity.
The garden has famous topiary work (the trees are a bit
like chessmen) and the potting shed roof has finials of
romping monkeys along its ridge. There's an old sundial
and a rather superior doocot dated 1599.

The Bruce family of Earlshall probably built the castle in the days of James IV. The second laird lived through the reigns of James IV, James V, Mary and James VI. He fought at Flodden and died with James VI the acknowledged heir to the united kingdoms. His tombstone is in Leuchars Church, dated 1584, declaring Sir William had died in his 98th year. *Mors omnium est finis*. A later laird was an ardent ally of Claverhouse. He butchered Richard Cameron, the hardline Covenanter, at Aird's Moss and captured Hackston, one of the assassins of Archbishop Sharp, who was then barbarously executed in Edinburgh. After James VII went into exile he became a Whig. His son left only daughters and Earlshall went to the Hendersons of Fordell by marriage, after which it went through many owners. Mary Queen of Scots stayed at Earlshall, of course. (All monarchs in those days moved round their realms: which meant free D, B&B and allowed them to keep an eye on their nobles.)

Robert Mackenzie, a bleach merchant from Dundee, bought the castle in 1890. His peers thought him daft, but he knew exactly what he wanted, and he engaged the young Lorimer to restore the building we have today. In 1926 he sold the estate to Sir Michael Nairn, the Kirkcaldy linoleum tycoon, who gave it to his daughter as a wedding present.

Past the castle we skirt the airfield perimeter briefly (by Comerton Farm), then when the track swings left (to a cycle-cross race track), head straight on through a small wood. There's a graveyard of old farm machinery, then the track skirts outside another bit of plantation.

The track turns hard right at the end of the plantation and 150m on, left, the FCP goes through two pedestrian gates and along a fence-enclosed walkway. (This is to protect walkers from cattle!) After 150m turn right, following a field edge, to the boggy open woodland. There are duckboards. Lots of duckboards. Eventually turn left through a long waymarked grassy glade in the scattered woodland and, at the far end, a bridge leads into **Tentsmuir Forest** proper.

Head on along the forestry track to reach the small tarmac Leuchars-Kinshaldy Beach road, a track labelled Canal Loch Road at the junction. Turn right. Shortly after, the Polish Camp road goes off on the left and could

Kinshaldy road in Tentsmuir Forest

be taken for Tayport in an emergency to cut out the Tentsmuir circuit.

Continuing, we come on a fine beech tree avenue, which leads to Kinshaldy.

This is an area of delightful wildness, rich in birds, insects and flowers. There is no shortage of skylarks here–or on many days along the coast. Look out for gaudy cinnabar moth caterpillars crowding on ragwort. Last time here I came up to within fifteen yards of a fox and spent twenty minutes watching it hunt through the long grass, unaware of my presence. When it did scent me it was off in a flash. One Tentsmuir snag–be warned–in high summer there can be a horrible plague of flies.

Kinshaldy Riding Stables (Tel: 01334-838527) lie just off to the right, and ponies will be seen in the few fields islanded in the oceanic spread of Tentsmuir Forest. A kilometre on the road ends at the popular Kinshaldy beach carpark, where there are picnic tables, toilets, display boards etc. (Motorists are charged a small fee to park.)

Tentsmuir Forest goes back to 1922, planting on what was basically salt marshes at the NE corner of Fife. The Stewart kings once hunted bears in its wilds, and shipwrecked sailors and all manner of broken men hid in its fastness. Salmon fishing eventually brought some respectability to the coast. The NE corner of forest and the dunes are a National Nature Reserve. The trees are mostly Scots pine, many mature, so there is no feeling of claustrophobia as broad tracks and coastal paths take us on to the Tay.

You can continue north through the forest on a broad track or walk along the sands as far as the Nature Reserve boundary, where a path will lead back to the track and the Southern Reserve entrance (each entrance has notice boards and interpretative displays). Wandering into the reserve should be avoided, as the wildlife should not be disturbed and dunes are fragile features. Mesolithic people roamed the sea's edge 8000 years ago. A dug-out canoe has been found, and heaps of shells from eating places which were then by the sea, now by the road from Leuchard to Tayport.

The main attraction on the track comes next: a large ice house, one of those half-sunken, grassed-over buildings where salmon etc could be kept fresh in summer. Ice was carted from the Highlands in winter months to ice houses all over Fife and Lowland Scotland. Fridges came rather later! On the other side of the track there is a choked pond where, if you approach quietly, you may see herons (and damsel flies). A track runs seawards to an old observation post; notices/information by the gate are interesting.

Tentsmuir has very diverse bird life; besides herons, moorhens and gulls here, there are wrens, green and great

Ice house in Tentsmuir Forest

spotted woodpeckers, sparrow hawks, curlews and war-blers. Other species abound: colourful snails, rabbits galore, foxes, roe deer and red squirrels. Go quietly and you may see some of these. Bat boxes have encouraged three species to live in the forest. Grey and common seals haul out on the remoter sandbanks. Butterflies abound. Highland cattle keep the vegetation under control by their grazing. Husky dogs are occasionally met in winter, for teams race in Scotland, but on wheels rather than sledge runners.

Continuing along the big track we come to a Y-junction with a well-endowed marker post. Take the right fork. After another stretch look out for a track going off at right angles to another gate into the reserve with the familiar notices. While the official route keeps on by the big track, it is much pleasanter to go up to this Great Slack Entrance, read what that entails and follow the footpath along the boundary past the wind pump. Slacks are wet hollows with a special flora and attract many insects (look out for the vivid burnet moths), and the wind pump helps keep the area flooded in winter. The grazing cattle help to prevent the dunes being taken over by seeding pines.

The line of wartime concrete blocks once stood at the high tide mark–now they are well inland, an extraordinary sight. (Some of the grains of sand could have originated on Ben Alder or Schiehallion or Ben Lui.) Tentsmuir gains ground eastwards by about five yards a year!

The path leads on to the final northern reserve entrance where there are more interpretive board s – reached through a gap in the fence. Here we are turning west into the Tay Estuary proper. We see the Sidlaw Hills behind Dundee, Broughty Ferry with its castle, Monifieth off the end of the tidal fence of the reserve, then the Barry Links (which hide Carnoustie) and right out to Buddon Ness. The sands offshore are the Green Scalp.

There are two options now. For all but the most timid, the path along the edge of the dunes (and/or going along the beach) will give the most interest (we are exploring the coast!) and this can be taken from below this point. The alternative is to continue along the path and then regain the big track, left, which is the official FCP/Cycle Way, but it does a great loop round away from the sea, through the regimented pines, and, ironically, ends along the shore for a stretch that can be swamped at the highest tides. Just before this juncture a direct track from Leuchars comes in (Leuchars 4½), the coast route back is given as 7, while, ahead, Tayport is 1¾ and the bridge 3½. There are machine gun posts up on the bank and a last scatter of anti-invasion blocks; along the beach here many are half-buried in the sand, as erosion is nibbling into the forest edge, a contrast to earlier. Offshore names appeal: Lucky Scalp, Tony Scalp, White Scalp, Tom's Hole, Snook Head... Lundin Bridge ends the Tentsmuir interest; ahead **Tayport** strings round to its harbours, where estuary narrows to become river, once a vital ferry site.

Keep to the green area of the links and then walk through the Tayport caravan park to a further green area with a shelter, right, and playing fields and a large pond, left. Near the end of the esplanade, take the footpath on the seawall which runs along the back of the houses and pops out at the yacht-busy harbour. (In really rough weather turn right at the end of the esplanade and follow Harbour Road.) Offshore lies a pile lighthouse, built in 1848 when the Tay was busy with whaling vessels. It looks a bit like 'a dalek on stilts'.

Tayport Harbour as we see it dates to 1847, and was constructed as the Fife terminal for the Edinburgh and Northern Railway ferry, one imitating the Burntisland-Leith 'floating railway'. The older village of Ferryport-on-Craig took on new life as a result. The rail

Tayport Harbour

bridge has rather eclipsed Tayport (while Newport, Woodhaven and Wormit prospered) but a ferry over to Broughty Ferry operated till 1939. Historically this was the crossing taken by drovers heading south. Broughty Castle indicates its strategic importance; the castle on this side has disappeared, the only hint in the name Castle Street.

Walk round the harbour to a parking area. Inland lie the Bell Rock Tavern with its gable mural and Jane's Harbour Tea Room. Broad Street, between, runs up into the town centre. Tayport sprawls with many wynds and secretive corners and plenty of architectural interest, but exploring is not likely to appeal at this stage, afoot anyway. A display board points out that President Ulysses S Grant crossed the Tay ferry and made a point of studying Bouch's new (not yet disastrous) rail bridge.

Continue along to the West Shore where there's another harbour/slip and turn left through a court of attractive modern houses built to blend with more traditional styles. A red gravel footway leads through a barrier of posts, then, immediately after, turn right on a path between walls. This leads out to a grassy area with two remaining bridges–now like parallel walls–marking the line of the old railway which we walk for about a mile and a half.

The Cycle Way drops down a small tarred road. Don't take this, nor the broad track for the houses, but start from the west side of the small car park and aim left of the wall above the small tarred road. The path soon becomes obvious. There are two breaks where bridges have been removed, giving down-and-ups on the seaward side (hence cyclists using the road). Two lighthouses stand on the shore, built by Robert Stevenson. Originally identical, the eastern is now derelict, the west rebuilt and painted white, a notable sea mark. There's a good view of it just past the second path down-and-up, then the route rises steadily, first through a pleasant tree avenue and then open farmland, to reach the B946. Dundee now fills the view, some of the tower blocks looking as high as the Law.

The Cycle Way/FCP now runs along parallel with, and just below, the B946, with only one parking loop interruption. When it ends, take great care crossing the B946 to go up the bridge road (only 50 yards) and right into the car park area whence a footpath leads to the **Tay Bridge**. A more interesting and perhaps safer option is to follow the B946 pavement under the bridge, then cross the road, and take steps up to reach the pedestrian access to the bridge. The pedestrian/ cyclists' track lies in the middle of the bridge, between the vehicle lanes, an odd feeling after the Forth Road Bridge.

The road bridge was opened by the Queen Mother in 1966 and must be regarded as func-

West Light, Tayport

tional rather than fascinating. (North east Fife's water main comes over it in a 24-inch pipeline.) There's a dramatic obelisk marking the roundabout at the south end and the bridge's lines are not unattractive. Walking across is a good way to finish. In the centre of the walkway the tiles are laid out in the pattern of the knight's move in chess: the architect was a champion player.

Two miles upstream is the railway bridge (slightly larger) which crosses to Wormit, while between the two bridges the south shore is continuously built-up: Newport-onTay, Woodhaven, Wormit, with Pluck the Crow Point central. The Tay Bridge is always thought of in connection with the disaster of 1879 when Sir Thomas Bouch's original single-track bridge collapsed during a violent storm, taking a train with it and killing 75 people. A bridge of over two miles across the Tay estuary was an ambitious project and Bouch was perhaps unlucky to be a pioneer. The cause is still debated, but basically the bridge was too frail–which is why the Forth Bridge was made so immensely strong. The present double-track bridge was begun in 1882 (Engineers, W H Barlow; contractor, W Arrol). It recycled some of the original girders and was completed in 1887, when it was the longest rail

Tay Road Bridge

bridge in the world (and is still the longest in Europe). The foundations of the first bridge lie along the seaward side of the new like gigantic stepping stones. Walking across the road bridge, if nothing else, gives a feeling of the scale of the estuary.

Before the bridge was built, Thomas Telford's 1823 steamboat pier was Newport's link with Dundee. The rich industrialists built their elegant villas and mansions on the Fife shore, well away from the grime and din–so commuting is not a new phenomenon. It was also Dundee's bathing resort. Near the harbour one of the decorative cast-iron milestones that mark routes across East Fife declares 'Newport 0' while the highly ornate canopied drinking fountain (1882) is both striking and beautiful. The 1966 road bridge finally ended ferry services across the Tay.

Dundee, Scotland's historic fourth city, is a good place to finish our walk round the Fife Coast, bridges to bridges. Crowded between the volcanic plug of the Law and the Tay (120 miles from its source), the old town has been transformed many times, but much of interest lies within short walking distance of the road bridge and some further explorations may appeal before travelling homewards. Accommodation is plentiful.

Probably the most outstanding 'extra' is a visit to Discovery Point, where Captain Scott's *RRS Discovery* (built in Dundee) will already have caught the eye from the

Tay Railway Bridge

bridge. Next door is the Olympia Leisure Centre (big swimming pool, climbing wall etc) and nearby the oldest warship afloat, the frigate *Unicorn*. In the city centre, (Albert Square) is the striking McManus Galleries with strong representation of Victorian/Twentieth-century British art, McTaggart and Patrick, besides specialities on pre-history, wildlife and the Tay Bridge disaster. The award-winning Dundee Contemporary Arts complex is very popular, as is the Perth Rep Theatre. (There are also three other theatres.) Using all modern presentation skills are the Verdant Works (featuring jute and the industrial past) and Sensation, the 'live science' centre. The Law (174m/571 feet) is a great viewpoint, and on Balgay Hill the Mills Observatory is open to the public. The Howff, an historic graveyard in the town centre, has typical craft symbol stones. There are many churches of architectural interest. The Old Steeple can be climbed. Shaw's Sweet Factory is an unusual visitor attraction. North of the city is the huge Camperdown Country Park and there is a Botanic Garden (on Riverside Drive). Details of all these can be obtained from the Tourist Office in Castle Street.

Dundee, lying on the east coast route to Aberdeen, has had a stormy history even by Scottish standards and has always had a certain pioneering spirit. It was once Britain's chief whaling port, and a hub of the textile industry. The old saying of 'Jute, Jam and Journalism' was certainly true. A Mrs Keillor invented marmalade and D C Thomson remains firmly in the city–producers of everything from the *Beano* and *Dandy* to *The Scots Magazine* (which dates back to 1739). The city has always had strong medical connections with both research and production, which continue to this day. Dundee is also very much a student centre (with 39,000 students), including the notable Duncan of Jordanstone College of Art.

Dundee Railway Station lies only 450 yards from the bridge (on the up-river side) while the Bus Station is in the Seagate near the town centre but, having walked both road bridges, the aesthetic finale has to be catching the train to Edinburgh to cross both railway bridges. The journey is a pleasant one, from the seasweep of Tay, through rolling north east Fife, the Howe of Fife, past the Lomond Hills and then reeling in the Fife coast from Kirkcaldy to the greatest bridge of them all to leave the Kingdom. We can quote both Eliot, 'In my beginning is my end', and Mary Queen of Scots, 'In my end is my beginning'. Haste ye back.

Appendix I
Inchcolm and Inchkeith

INCHCOLM

Inch is just another Gaelic-originated Scots word for *island* with the Forth Estuary and Loch Lomond having popular clusterings of the word. Inchcolm is Columba's Isle, Colm being another form of the saint's name. (Inchkeith is likewise Keith's Island.) One of the island's earliest (true) incidents has a mention in Shakespeare's *Macbeth*: Sueno, defeated by Macbeth at Kinghorn, is allowed to bury his dead on Inchcolm–for a big fee. A strange hogsback grave dates to that period.

The island is famous for its abbey, which has survived better than most, its island setting being a defence both against attack and the pillaging of its stones (think of St Andrews cathedral!) Alexander I was caught in a storm crossing the Forth in 1123 and vowed, if saved, to found an abbey in St Columba's name. His craft reached the island and he was provided for by a hermit who lived in a cell, a 'desert' (from which the name Dysart), which still survives. David I (Alexander's brother) founded a priory which became an abbey a century later. Sir William Mortimer, Aberdour landowner, fell out with the monks but nevertheless gave half his lands and an endowment

Inchcolm Abbey

to ensure he was buried on the holy island. Somehow, on the crossing, his lead coffin went overboard; hence the name Mortimer's Deep off Braefoot, where the supertankers benefit from the deep water.

Columba's name was obviously one to be respected. English raiders in 1335 bore off abbey treasures, only to be overtaken by a storm off Inchkeith, so they pleaded with the saint for mercy, promising restitution. The storm abated and they landed the pillaged goods at Kinghorn. Another raid penetrated to the Ochils and went off with Dollar church goods. Not having interceded with the saint the ship sank in Mortimer's Deep–and Dollar parish church was dedicated to St Columba. English incursions were of a more serious nature during Henry VIII's 'Rough Wooing', when the monks evacuated the vulnerable island and, soon after, the Reformation brought its end, the last old monk dying in 1578. The abbey however is the most complete ruin of its kind in Scotland (though Edinburgh's tolbooth is made from its stolen masonry). In 1854 workers found a skeleton standing upright within a wall of the Abbot's House.

Several times, like Inchkeith, the island was used as a convenient quarantine station. Before modern times infectious diseases were rightly feared. In 1845 a fleet visit of the Russian navy of Czar Nicholas I saw many sailors left there to die of a fever. About 1582 the *William of Leith* brought plague from England and was banned to the island, where most of the crew perished. Excavations have come on huge numbers of interments.

Many ruins are obviously dating to World War II (and some to World War I, or the Napoleonic period) and the best viewpoint, up on the eastern end, is one such site, with a clear prospect over the island and the pretty abbey. A boom (during World War II) was stretched from Inchcolm across to Cramond Island on the Lothian shore. All the *inches* were heavily armed, like static warships anchored in the firth. Inchmickery's buildings were intentionally made to look like a warship.

Do make sure of climbing to the top of the abbey tower (which had its upper floors as a doocot) though those of noble girth will find it a bit of a squeeze. A rare thirteenth-century mural painting has been discovered in the chancel, showing a procession of robed figures, censers swinging, though sadly the top section (with their heads) is missing. The island is green and pleasant, with little bays and quiet corners, and time seems to slow down to reward the visitor. Summer sailings allow access and Inchcolm is in the care of Historic Scotland.

The Walking

First call is the Visitor Centre, where the Historic Scotland custodian will give a briefing and can answer queries. There's a small exhibition, shop and toilet facilities. The main area is landscaped with lawns and gardens and some surprisingly big trees, with the abbey astride the narrow neck of the island. Walkers will want to reach the two extremities.

Heading towards the abbey, bear over to the right to pass the ruins and then head upwards. A path is kept open, for the ground, free of those four-legged lawnmowers called sheep, is rank with grass, cow parsley, nettles and shrubs. These quieter ends of the island have been taken over by black-backed gulls which will yell 'No! No!' at you and, as like as not, attack intruders.

There's a definite hillock that marks the highest furthest out point of easy access. Rafts of puffin are often seen on Mortimer's Deep. Return by the same route and pass right of the Visitor Centre to go up steps to the surprise of a tunnel. Through this the path leads on to the other extremity which has a light. Twist down steps and swing right for a traverse path back to base. This gives the best view of the abbey and is my favourite spot for a quick snack and drink.

INCHKEITH

Inchkeith has no tourist service running out to it, so a visit would depend on private arrangements or chartering. The island counts as part of Kinghorn parish, but the population is entirely gulls which, scavenging in refuse tips, are often suffering various fatal epidemics (botulism, etc). There is also a population of puffins. A good harbour makes landing easy enough, once there. Weekend yachts are the main visitors today, their spray-painted graffiti an eyesore. With the mixture of ruins, jungle and gulls Inchkeith is no beauty spot.

The king Malcolm II, hard-pressed by Danish attacks, rewarded the northerner, Robert de Keith, with the island for his help in fending off the Vikings, and though it didn't remain long in the Earl Marischal family, the name has stuck. Through the centuries it has been a fortress of one sort or another. Since the government sold it off there have been attempts at having it as an animal sanctuary, a children's playground or an exclusive Edinburgh commuters' resort. The next daft idea is about due.

James IV housed a dumb woman with two children on Inchkeith to see what, if anything, they would learn to speak. Both 'languages of God' (Hebrew and Gaelic) were claimed, but the truth was they didn't speak any language as such.

Many lighthouse experiments were made on the island, such as introducing the dioptric system, but in 1899 when the foghorn was installed it sounded non-stop for 130 hours, which nearly drove Fife residents crazy. It was then turned to face out to sea. Today the friendly roar has gone and the light is automatic. Despite these aids a fisheries cruiser, the *Switha* 'took the ground' in 1980 and is still a stark landmark off the SE corner.

Inchkeith was the first light built solely by Robert Stevenson of the famous engineering family, in 1804. The Bell Rock (off the Tay, 1811) and the May Island (further out in the Forth, 1816) were also his. A Thomas Smith began this four-generation connection with lighthouses. In the late eighteenth century life was precarious, and he lost several children and two wives before finally marrying a lady, herself twice widowed and the mother of Robert Stevenson, who became Smith's partner and successor and married one of Smith's daughters as well. Their sons, Alan, David and Thomas (father of R.L.S.) were all lighthouse engineers, as were David's two sons, one of whose sons only died in 1971. Kirkcaldy, Leven, Anstruther, Crail and St Andrews all have Stevenson harbour works. Thomas Smith made his fortune from lighting the streets of Edinburgh. He fitted out an Elie-built sloop for the Northern Lights Trust and the name *Pharos* has been used by the changing service ever since.

Appendix 2
Largo Law

Largo Law, at 290m. (952ft.) may not be a big hill, but its isolated stance above the Forth makes it a grandstand viewpoint and a climb is recommended, either as part of the coastal walk or at another time. The only recognised route is from the primary school on a minor road leading inland from Upper Largo, itself with some historical interests.

If aiming for Largo Law from Lower Largo, turn off at the noted signpost: 'Serpentine Walk to Upper Largo'. This path crosses the old coastal railway route before wending up a den (dell) under the care of the Woodlands Trust to reach the A915 coastal road, which is followed up, right, into Upper Largo. The black and white cottages (featuring rusticated quoins), off right, are a striking feature. Facing the path exit onto the A915 are the eagle-topped pillars of a gateway, with the 1750 John Adam mansion standing derelict up beyond. The road swings sharp right at the *Yellow Carvel*. Immediately after Path House on the left is the minor road we follow.

Upper Largo is also Kirkton of Largo and the church, left, has a Pictish stone at the entrance with a hunting scene and one of the mysterious 'swimming beasts'. A

Largo Law

gravestone at the side of the church has El Greco-like elongated figures and a sad story to tell. Continuing up the wee road (North Feus) there are a couple more pie- bald cottages and, looking over the wall opposite, a hollow is seen curving across a field towards a pepperpot tower. This is the course of the first-ever canal cut in Scot- land, in the fifteenth century, for Sir Andrew Wood, local chiel and naval hero, who was rowed to church in his admiral's barge by captured English sailors. Wood was a successful merchant who had proved his capabilities against pirates and enemy attacks, so James III made him admiral. He also served the brilliant James IV. Early in the latter's reign, though not at war, five armed English merchantmen attacked shipping in the Forth. Wood, with just two ships, captured all five. Henry VIII was not amused and sent Stephen Bull with three ships of war to capture or destroy Wood. Wood, returning from Flanders with the *Yellow Carvel* and *Flower*, was attacked off the May and the battle raged all day and night, ending off Fife Ness with Bull's surrender. The crews were repatri- ated–after the lower deck prisoners dug his canal. Wood oversaw the construction of the *Great Michael* (much big- ger than the *Mary Rose*) whose building devastated Fife's woods. The pepperpot tower (doocot at one state) is all that remains of the castle he built. He is buried in the church.

Another (John) Wood (a descendant), who died in 1681, had been a royalist courtier and left quite a fortune for a *hospital* (hospice) for 'indigent and enfeebled men'–who had to bear the name Wood. Rebuilt in the 1830s in Jaco- bean mansion style, the building still offers sheltered housing for the elderly, but no longer all having to have the same surname.

Just past the primary school is the parking place which has notices about the ascent of Largo Law. The route edges a field, passes a row of neatly restored cottages and goes on to Chesterstone Farm, in and out the yard and round the back to turn sharp left, uphill, as a green track aiming straight at Largo Law. Rough pasture with gorse leads steeply up the final cone above the arable level. Cows may be grazing, so observe the country code. There's a false top, then a dip (with a stile over a fence), to reach the 290m. trig point, the highest point along the Fife coast and a notable viewpoint. Retrace the upward route exactly back to the primary school.

If the start was made at Lower Largo a good circular walk is possible rather than just backtracking. Turn right on joining the wee road past the school, and opposite the cemetery gates go left along a field edge path, to come out at another minor road, which is crossed to go over and down into Keil's Den, another Woodlands Trust dell. This is followed down, then left, to exit to the minor road crossed earlier. Turn down to cross the A915 back to Lower Largo (150 metres, right, along the A915 is a pleasant tearoom/restaurant).

Appendix 3
The Chain Walk

The Chain Walk (created in 1929) is a potentially dangerous undertaking, involving dangling across cliffs on chains, sometimes above the sea, with strenuous ascents and descents. It is not practical at high tide, and a start should only be made from half ebb to half flow. An hour at least is needed to complete the route. In many places bucket steps have been cut, but weathering has made some of these precarious, and the rock is greasy when wet. There are no escape routes. Treat the fun passage seriously; it is a unique entertainment. You tackle it at your own risk!

For the start of this refer to p.76. If coming from Earlsferry (on a separate occasion) the start is best reached by walking over Kincraig Hill or parking at Shell Bay (for a small charge) and traverse back over Kincraig Hill after the Chain Walk.

On descending the initial slope to rock level you'll see a rectangular cave set in the back of a cove to the right: the Devil's Cave, which runs in a surprising distance. The approach is by a shallow gully seawards, so only practical at low tide. The Chain Walk is round to the left from the zigzag descent. Don't drop too far down as easier ground tempts, but keep a higher traverse which leads to the first short chain down into a cove (one shallow, one deeper cave), then a traverse of cliff with horizontal chains for security. This leads to a vertical chain in a corner, the longest haul upwards, but eased by cut steps once above the overhanging start. There's an iron post on the neck at the top.

Beyond is a beach with a huge inter-tide flat area marked with lines of dykes so straight they look man-made. There are pinnacles and spikes worn out of the breccias of the point and the sea surges in deep cut gullies. The flat area ends at Kincraig Point itself. A wall of organ-pipes (columnar basalt) will entertain, then there is another vertical chain to haul up, then we head down the other side into a wee bay where we swing left to a marked neck in another lava-flow. A short chain leads

On the Chain Walk

down to the major area of geological interest. There's a big spread of soaring basalt pillars above a 'scree' of disintegrated hexagonal pieces. A huge grouping of pillars is detached and leans precariously against the main wall. Beyond, the sea-sculpted stumps of long-gone pillars have weathered into what looks a bit like a limestone pavement. The grey shingle has been tumbled into appealing smoothness, often nesting in sea-hollows in the rocks.

From the far top end of the shingle, steps lead up to traverse along the rocks and round a point. Large steps lead down to one of those strange flat areas. Head up left of a natural arch. (Except at low tide it does not offer a way through.) The cliffs are at their most impressive above, beetling out in big bellyfolds of rock, noisy with fulmars in the first half of the year.

The next (last) cove is the most serious. Look across at the far side: horizontal chains (with steps cut) lead out to a ledge and down to a lower one–which, at low tide, can be reached from the beach by big steps. The innermost chain can be avoided too but, at high tide, the water will be over the steps in the rock. The way down into the cove is the crux of the whole venture, and can be rather intimidating. One traverses down and along, to step then across a gap onto a detached fin of rock in the cove itself. There are excellent handholds and technically it is not difficult with care. Lean well out so you can spot the holds; cringing in simply constricts and blinds. Avoid the back of the cove (where there are fallen rocks) and go along the horizontal chains as much as the tide dictates or the spirit moves. When the chain ends the route is *down*, on steps almost weathered away, easiest taken facing in. The lower ledge can be slippery. And that is it! Easy going leads down to the warm red sands of Earlsferry.

Appendix 4
May Island

The May is a renowned Nature Reserve with a residential observatory. A Scottish Natural Heritage warden will meet visiting boats, while there are plenty of leaflets and booklets on the interesting island, usually reached from Anstruther. (Publications are to be found in the Fisheries Museum.) There are daily sailings (on the *May Princess*) in the summer months, weather permitting, and times may vary depending on the state of the tide. Usually three hours ashore is given. If taken in during walking the coast, it is satisfying to know the Isle of May lies 56km./35 miles east of the Forth Bridge. It is a tilted slab of basalt with stark, dark cliffs.

David I (the deeply religious king) gave the island to the Berkshire Benedictine monastery of Reading, but it had a stormy history of pillage and natural harshness, and when it was transferred to the see of St Andrews following the Battle of Bannockburn (1314) the monks transferred to Pittenweem and the island's ecclesiastical importance disappeared. Only recently have archaeologists been investigating these years of occupancy. The Northern Lighthouse Commission purchased the May in 1815 and Robert Stevenson built the present handsome light in the centre of the island in 1816.

Next to it are the lower parts of the seventeenth-century light. Once higher, it had a grate on top where a fire beacon consumed a ton of coal per night and needed constant attention. Shipping had to pay for this service, the first of its kind anywhere in Scotland. The cinders piled up round the building with tragic results, for, no light showing, investigation found the keeper, his wife and five children all dead in their beds from carbon monoxide poisoning. The very first keeper drowned in a storm, and a poor Anstruther woman was accused of causing this and strangled and burnt as a witch.

The Low Light dates to 1843, and, with the main light, allowed a fix on the treacherous Carr Rocks off Fife Ness. Despite the lights, the century past has seen 39 ships wrecked on the May. The Latvian *Mars* (wrecked in North

Ness on what are now Mars Rocks) and the Danish *Island* (at Colmshole) are still visible hulks. The latter was once the Danish royal yacht.

Many visitors are particularly interested in birds, and a regular programme of ringing and other studies is maintained. The main observatory was established in 1934. The May is often the first spring or autumn landfall for migrants. Well over 200 species have been recorded. A kittiwake ringed on the May was recovered in Newfoundland, a robin in Spain; conversely, finds include a sparrowhawk ringed in Iceland and a goldcrest ringed in Finland, less than a month before.

The May (which may be the Norse word for *gull*) could be renamed Puffin Island. There are something like 84,000 of these comics, plus a back-up of 2,000 terns, 26,000 guillemots, 3,500 razorbills, 1,000 shags, 800 fulmars, 10,000 kittiwakes and 9,000 gulls. The decibel level on the cliffs is considerable. The puffins are everywhere, a great delight. Many years ago I took a school gang to the May. On the way back I noticed the donkey jacket sleeve of one boy was bulging–and moving. A somewhat bedraggled puffin was shaken out and flew off home, hell for feather.

The Walking

There is a great web of marked paths, on which visitors are asked to remain, and what follows is simply one option. The Visitor Centre has leaflets with a map. On landing at the reef-held Kirkhaven, a ranger will give a welcome/briefing. Head up quickly to the Visitor Centre for a map, then on up to pass the impressive building of the Main Light and keep along the spine of the island. Ignore a track, off right, which descends to the Low Light (now an observatory). Descend to a hut and, on the left, lies the Altarstanes landing, held between bird-noisy cliffs. A bridge leads across onto Rona and the North Horn. (The horns are no longer operational; the pipes one sees along the way carried compressed air to them.)

Wend back again and on the slope to the Main Light, turn right, into Three Tarns Nick, to reach the cliff edge at Bishop Cove. If you approach very slowly and sit still you can watch puffins mere yards away. The sheer cliffs

Puffins on the May Island

here are impressive, every niche a nest, the whole white
with guano. Return to the main path but shortly break
off again to curve up to the Main Light. The keepers'
walled gardens have one of the Heligoland bird traps and
one optimistically has been planted with trees.

Escape down beside the building and then right, taking a narrow path by a wall, to reach the pea-green loch
and old lighthouse establishment. Out from it, the Visitor Centre might be looked at if not crowded, then go

past the Kirkhaven landing and on, taking the left options, finally to circuit round to the South Horn. Keep on circuiting to reach Pilgrims Haven, the only beach on the island, a good corner for some refreshments, with a windbreak wall, pipe to sit on, and a view to seastacks and cliffs.

Keep along by the wall to reach the now excavated site of the early religious settlement, and so back to the Visitors' Centre. The *May Princess* carries a maximum 100 passengers, so there is no feeling of being crowded on the island. In summer the slopes can be snowy white with sea campion, thrift nods from the lichened rocks, the sea shimmers and there are vast skyscapes.

Appendix 5
Chart of Distances

Distances are *in miles* and are approximations, and give
the basic, shortest options. Side visits and the complex
wanderings of the FCP will certainly push the distances
higher. (The accumulative 67 miles is 107 kilometres.)

	Distance *miles*	Accumulated **Distance** *miles*
Dalmeny–Queensferry	1.0	
Forth Bridge	1.5	2.5
N. Queensferry–Inverkeithing	2.0	4.5
Inverkeithing–Aberdour	4.5	9.0
Aberdour–Burntisland	2.0	11.0
Burntisland–Kinghorn	2.0	13.0
Kinghorn–Kirkcaldy, start	2.0	15.0
In Kirkcaldy–Dysart	2.5	17.5
Dysart–East Wemyss	3.5	21.0
East Wemyss–Buckhaven	1.5	22.5
Buckhaven–Leven	2.0	24.5
Leven–Lower Largo	2.0	26.5
Lower Largo–Earlsferry	2.5	29.0
Earlsferry/Elie	1.0	30.0
Elie–St Monans	2.5	32.5
St Monans–Pittenweem	1.5	34.0
Pittenweem–Anstruther (Fisheries Museum)	1.0	35.0
Anstruther–Crail	3.5	38.5
Crail–Fife Ness	2.5	41.0
Fife Ness–Kingsbarns (coastal car park)	3.0	44.0
Kingsbarns–Buddo Rock	3.5	47.5
Buddo Rock–Central St Andrews	3.5	51.0
St Andrews–Guardbridge	3.5	53.5
Guardbridge–Kinshaldy (car park)	5.0	58.5
Kinshaldy–Lundin Bridge	5.0	63.5
Tayport–Tay Bridge	3.5	67.0